Ditch Depression Devotional:

31 Days to Biblical Hope, Peace and Emotional Balance

Jody Shee

All Scriptures quoted from the KJV Bible

ISBN-13: 978-0692306789

Purple
dreamer
Publishers

DEVOTIONAL

This devotional is designed to be completed in one month, but is also appropriate for use in a classroom or small-group setting with assignments at the end of each chapter. A free online leader's guide dividing the book into sections is available at mastertruth.com.

Contents

INTRODUCTION

When you're at work, school or church, out shopping, eating, or just hanging out with friends, you see a carefully guarded, polished side of those around you that likely doesn't even closely represent reality. You would be amazed if you saw the default setting in the minds and hearts of your comrades. They hide it well. It's the social norm to appear like a sane functioning adult. And that is probably a good thing, because who wants to cope with the inner wrangling of others when you have your own to deal with?

I have a hunch that many people, perhaps even you, walk around with low-grade depression with fluctuating spikes and reprieves. You wouldn't tell people that. It's just not something you talk about. But it's always there.

The severity of depression can be a result of many things, including hormones and other physical and mental maladies, some of which would be well-served by the guidance of a professional.

Your God-given temperament also plays a role in your natural emotional fortitude. You may wish you were cheerful and unaffected by rocky turbulence as others appear to be, but that's just not realistic. (Avoid comparing your insides with other people's outsides.)

Fortunately, the topic of depression is widely covered in the Bible. And so, we are going on a month-long devotional journey together. We're going to quit being secretive about depression so we can perfect the mental, emotional and spiritual tools to deal with it.

When you are done with this book, you will have replaced heaviness and despair with comfort, hope, peace and purpose. You will learn to turn to God and the Bible instead of chocolate and potato chips (or worse, drugs and alcohol). You'll come face to face with who you are, followed by an enriching look at who God is and then a look at several Bible characters and how they dealt with situations that could have left them in a depressed stupor.

The most effective way to traverse this book is to go one day at a time. Don't be reading ahead. Sufficient for the day is the reading and pondering of the chapter thereof.

To begin, the 1913 edition of "Webster's Dictionary," defines *depressed* as "pressed or forced down; lowed; sunk; dejected; dispirited; sad; humbled." Who doesn't relate to those words?

PART 1: SOBER MINDED

For the first nine days, let's examine some thoughts, feelings, viewpoints and attitudes that are recipes for depression. The Bible encourages us to be sober minded. *Young men likewise exhort to be sober minded.* (Titus 2:6) Sober minded means to be of sound mind, or be in one's right mind. Goodness. Do we need to be told to be in our right minds? Apparently so, and it's the key to overcoming depression. Rather than listen to our thoughts, we need to purposefully direct our thoughts.

Here's a profound summary of the concept of being in your right mind: *Now the first thing you have to do is take a firm grip of yourself, to pull yourself up, to stir up yourself, to take yourself in hand and to speak to yourself. As the Apostle puts it, we have to remind ourselves of certain things.* (D. Martyn Lloyd-Jones from the book "Spiritual Depression: Its Causes and Its Cures"—1965, see Appendix 2).

So that's the goal of Part 1. You will look at some of your natural dispositions that lead you down the path to depression, and you will consider the Biblical thinking that will turn you around and face you in the right direction.

Day 1: Selfishness Has No Purpose

S elfishness or self-centeredness is one of the strongest poisons of the heart leading to depression. We were born as "me-monsters." We learned as babies how to get attention and secure whatever we want to make us comfortable. It's something we don't automatically unlearn. We grow up thinking that life is about pleasure. That means we must always be comfortable, happy and fulfilled. Isn't that what we want for our children? Wouldn't that be what God wants for us as His children?

Actually, life's purpose is about God's pleasure. *Thou art worthy, O Lord, to receive glory and honour and power: for thou hast created all things, and for thy pleasure they are and were created.* (Rev. 4:11)

The first step in turning your thought and emotional life around is to realize that you weren't created for yourself. God is at the center of the universe, not you. Determine to make decisions and plans around God's pleasure and not your own. As you grow in spiritual maturity from reading your Bible each day and praying, you will grasp all that this means.

For now, realize that selfishness is akin to living life as a practical atheist. God is not in all your thoughts. *You* are in all your thoughts.

Beware that you don't go through another day tuned in only to your own thoughts and feelings with no regard for God's thoughts and instructions. *A fool hath no delight in understanding, but that his heart may discover itself.* (Prov.18:2)

You can tell if you are plagued with self-centeredness if you have an unthankful disposition. Thankfulness focuses your thoughts outside of yourself to God. Make thankful thoughts of praise a daily priority.

Look at Psalm 103 for inspiration. David praises God for forgiveness of sins; for God's lovingkindness and tender mercies; for good things to eat; that God is slow to anger; and for God's righteousness.

Turn your eyes upward. Look out the window and notice how faithful God is in causing the sun to rise each day and set each evening. He does it without fail. He gives the birds and squirrels food to eat every day, for His pleasure. He made sea creatures in the ocean depths that no human has ever seen, for His pleasure. This is the thought direction in which God took Job when He finally spoke to the dear depressed man in Job 38 after Job's friends had advised him how to think—incorrectly. His friends tried to make him be introspective, delving into all his actions, inactions and failings. But here's the point: God wanted Job to be extrospective. Job's friends tempted him to look in. Society and pop-psychology always advise you to look inward. But God says to look up. Read Job 38 and notice all the questions God asked Job. None of those questions and answers were about Job. They were about God.

Back to your purpose. God made you as part of the highest form of earthly intelligence to recognize, acknowledge, praise, honor and serve Him. That's your purpose. Not to be happy, healthy, wealthy and fulfilled. Be thankful for who God has made you to be and for the gifts He has given you that you can use for His glory and to the benefit of others.

How did He make you to honor Him? That is for you to discover. What can you do to bring Him glory? Start with your upward thoughts, your prayers, your desires and your ambitions. Ask Him what you can do for Him today. Start on a new adventure of selflessness with an aim to be an instrument to bring glory to God.

Going deeper:

■ If the whole idea of being God-centered sounds unappealing or foreign to you, consider whether or not you truly know God. Do you have a personal relationship with God through Jesus Christ that started when you recognized that you were separated from God by sin? Have you come to the end of yourself and recognized that to be right with God, you must acknowledge your sinful condition and accept Christ's death and resurrection for you? If not, learn more by going to Appendix 1.

■ Start a journal. Either buy one or start a new page on your computer. Each day for the next week, write five things you are thankful for, and consciously thank God. At first, you will likely thank God for the things around you that make you comfortable—your family, job, health, food on the table, etc. But then, branch out into marvelous aspects of God that you find in nature or from reading your Bible.

■ Read Psalm 103 and Job 38 and record any insights you receive.

■ Surrender your ambitions, hopes and plans to God before you go any further with this book. To help, talk to God through the song "Jesus, All for Jesus" written by Robin Mark and sung on YouTube. Simply type the song and singer information into YouTube.

Day 2: Anger is Ugly

Have you noticed that when you're angry, people tend to run away from you? You end up sitting on an island by yourself. *God* doesn't even want to be near you. That's not where you want to be. Leave anger to God for His righteous judgment.

Remember in the Old Testament when the Israelites were dying of thirst and they complained to Moses about it? God told Moses to strike the rock, and water would come out. Sure enough. Water came out, and the Israelites quenched their thirst. Then it happened again. This time God told Moses to *speak* to the rock and water would come out. (Start reading at Num. 20:7.) But Moses was angry with the people and he hit the rock twice. That's not what God asked him to do. Water came out again, and the Israelites drank.

But God was angry at Moses for being angry and disobeying Him. The consequences of that were severe. *And the LORD spake unto Moses and Aaron, because ye believed me not, to sanctify me in the eyes of the children of Israel, therefore ye shall not bring this congregation into the land which I have given them.* (Num. 20:12)

Moses, who was put on this earth to lead the Israelites into the Promised Land, didn't get to enter the Promised Land himself because of his anger and resulting disobedience. Surely that was depressing.

Anger takes a matter into its own hands and executes a verbal or physical punishment. The toll it takes on the other person is one thing, but the consequences to your own life in emotional-, physical- and relationship-grief are another. *Wherefore, my beloved brethren, let every man be swift to hear, slow to speak, slow to wrath: For the wrath of man worketh not the righteousness of God.* (James 1:19-20) *Dearly beloved, avenge not yourselves, but rather give place unto wrath: for it is written, Vengeance is mine; I will repay, saith the Lord.* (Rom. 12:19)

Learn to zip your lip. Give your flash fire or slow burn to God. After all, He's the one in control anyway. Let Him deal with the person or circumstance. Only God can work the righteousness of God. While He does that, your part is to forgive, sometimes over and over, like Jesus has to do for you.

Your emotional well-being depends on your ability to forgive and to turn grievances over to the Lord. *And grieve not the Holy Spirit of God, whereby ye are sealed unto the day of redemption. Let all bitterness, and wrath, and anger, and clamour, and evil speaking, be put away from you, with all malice: And be ye kind one to another, tenderhearted, forgiving one another, even as God for Christ's sake hath forgiven you.* (Eph. 4:30-32)

This indicates that anger isn't as much a feeling as it is a choice. You can put it away. Instead, you can choose to be kind and tenderhearted. It is possible.

Understand that your anger puts a wedge in your relationship with God and others. *If I regard iniquity in my heart, the Lord will not hear me:* (Psa. 66:18) Left unchecked, you end up depressed. *Be ye angry, and sin not: let not the sun go down upon your wrath.* (Eph. 4:26)

Going deeper:

■ Anger is just not how life is to be done. God doesn't operate in anger (Psa. 103:8), and He requires that we don't either. For further study on how we are to operate instead, read James 3:17-18; 2 Tim. 2:24-25; Prov. 14:29; 16:32; 19:11.

■ In your journal, write down the people and circumstances that either have you angry right now or that tend to cause your anger to flare. Is there some part of that you need to surrender to God? It's time to get on your knees about it. Do you need to make a decision to separate yourself from an individual or situation? Make that decision and separate yourself, if that's appropriate. Do you need to make things right with someone? Visit or call that person about it today before you chicken out. If there's someone you need to forgive but it seems too difficult, ask God to forgive that person through you.

Day 3: Loneliness is Not a Sin

Who can underestimate the depths of loneliness and its spiral into depression? It can easily and quickly lead to the emotional abyss. If you have ever experienced loneliness—caused by physical, emotional or spiritual isolation—I don't even need to describe the despair, and you don't need to be reminded.

The feeling of loneliness is not a sin that needs to be repented of. The first time the word *alone* is used in the Bible is Genesis 2:18 when God said, *It is not good that the man should be alone.* Thus He created a spouse for Adam.

I know what loneliness is and the depression it leads to. I was single until age 39, and not because I wanted to be single. Depression was almost unavoidable, but I always knew in my heart that God understood, and this time was only for a season. Things would get better.

If loneliness leads you to the depths of despair, just know that God is there. He understands. Remember when Jesus was left alone to face His darkest hour? Everyone turned away from Him, and He had to face the cross alone. He was more alone than anyone has ever been. You know the anguish He experienced wasn't entirely the physical pain of the cross. No. Remember what He cried out on the cross? *My God, My God. Why hast thou forsaken me? Forsaken* means abandoned or deserted. He was left alone—by God! He died of a broken heart, and maybe not solely for us, but also from the experience of being abandoned while He took on the sins of the world, and God turned away.

But he rose again. And now He's alive in heaven sitting at the right hand of God making intercession for you. *For we have not an high priest which cannot be touched with the feeling of our infirmities; but was in all points tempted like as we are, yet without sin.* (Heb. 4:15)

You can and should pray to Him and ask for relief. One of the things He has ordained that should help with loneliness is the body of Christ—the church.

I know, sometimes going to church alone is anguish. You might conclude that you will just worship God alone in your house or out in nature. You can do that. But you do need the church, because He gave spiritual gifts to His children, and when Christians all gather together in church exercising their gifts, they are like Christ and all He was. You need that. And the body of Christ needs you. Some in the body have the gift of exhortation, and you need to be around these kinds of people, just as they need the gifts you have, if you know Jesus as Savior. Everybody needs the body, not just you.

Loneliness is an emotional weakness, but not a sin. Ask God's help while you are weak.

Consider Paul's thorn in the flesh. God didn't take it away, but He taught Paul, *Therefore I take pleasure in infirmities, in reproaches, in necessities, in persecutions, in distresses for Christ's sake: for when I am weak, then am I strong.* (2 Cor. 12:10)

Loneliness is not comfortable, but God provides respites when you pray and ask. His strength can come out when you are weak. Ask Him for a dose of strength and relief today.

Going deeper:

■ If you are not part of a church, start praying and looking for one, trusting God's guidance. He has a place for you. Do a Google search for churches in your area, then check out some of their websites, including their doctrinal statement and the ministries they offer. Determine to visit a Bible-believing, Bible-preaching church each week until you find the one for you.

■ If you are part of a church, find a ministry you can get involved in with the goal of using your spiritual gifts. Remember the lesson from day 1: Your life is about glorifying God, not about you being comfy and happy. Getting involved in church is a determination you need to make, not a feeling you wait for. Take yourself in hand and put yourself out there.

■ Most importantly, you're never alone. Take a break, close your eyes and worship God to the song "Lord You Are Always Here With Me," written by Bo and Elsa Jarpehag. Type it into YouTube to listen to it.

Day 4: Bad Circumstances Happen to Good People

Nothing happens in your life outside of God's control. Do you believe that? If that's the case, why do bad things happen to people trying to live for the Lord? Everyone has probably asked that question when faced with a tragedy. That question comes in so many forms. Why would God create a person and then allow that person to go through unbearable suffering?

Job, who suffered as much as anyone, tried not to ask those questions, but those around him did, forcing him to engage in speculation. Was Job depressed? Yes, he was. But we know that God was near and was in control, even though it was Satan who asked for permission to make Job's life miserable:

Hast not thou made an hedge about him, and about his house, and about all that he hath on every side? Thou hast blessed the work of his hands, and his substance is increased in the land. But put forth thine hand now, and touch all that he hath, and he will curse thee to thy face. And the LORD said unto Satan, Behold, all that he hath is in thy power; only upon himself put not forth thine hand. So Satan went forth from the presence of the LORD. (Job 1:10-12) And after that, Job lost just about everything, except his wife, who told him to curse God and die.

It seems like a cruel experiment. But the bottom line is that God had His reasons. We know that He tries faith. *Wherein ye greatly rejoice, though now for a season, if need be, ye are in heaviness through manifold temptations: That the trial of your faith, being much more precious than of gold that perisheth, though it be tried with fire, might be found unto praise and honour and glory at the appearing of Jesus Christ.* (1 Pet. 1:6-7)

God was pleased with Job before the trial. He called him "my servant Job" two times before Job lost everything. And

God was pleased with Job *after* the trial, calling him "my servant Job" two times after it was all over in Job 42.

Look at the end of Job's trial, after his friends made his life even more miserable with their speculations and after God finally spoke and explained Himself to Job, *Job answered the LORD, and said, I know that thou canst do everything, and that no thought can be withholden from thee. Who is he that hideth counsel without knowledge? Therefore have I uttered that I understood not; things too wonderful for me, which I knew not. ...I have heard of thee by the hearing of the ear: but now mine eye seeth thee. Wherefore I abhor myself, and repent in dust and ashes.* (Job 42:1-6)

After the awesome God spoke to him, Job must have realized that he was merely a dot on a map and calendar. Who was he to question and figure out the God who transcends time and space?

Then, God had some words for Job's friends, who supposed they had divine insight into why all the bad things had happened to him: *The LORD said to Eliphaz the Temanite, My wrath is kindled against thee, and against thy two friends: for ye have not spoken of me the thing that is right, as my servant Job hath.* (Job 42:7)

What was the right thing Job had spoken? Paraphrased, he said, "God, you can do whatever you want, and no one can stop you. I talked about things I didn't understand. I see you now, and I am despicable in comparison. I repent."

You can't know why tragedy and suffering happens. Try not to theorize from your personal perspective when you find yourself having to muddle through disaster and heartbreak. Instead, hang on to God, who uses people and circumstances to accomplish His bigger, unknown-to-us eternal plans.

Going deeper:

■ Your circumstances might be undeniably bad, but God is undeniably good. I know a song that just might help your perspective today. Listen to this praise song by Don Moen, "God is Good." Simply search for that information on YouTube.

■ "Bad circumstances" are human words for God's word *trial*. Trials have a purifying purpose. Notice God's purpose and view of trials in these verses: 1 Pet. 4:12-13; Job 23:10; Psa. 66:10-12; Isa. 48:10; Rom. 5:3-4; James 1:3-4. Write down the ones you'd like to remember.

■ Are you still working on your thankful journal? If not, stop now and think of things you are thankful for and write them down. Make sure to thank God for them.

Day 5: Unfulfilled Expectations Aren't Limiting

You worked hard for a promotion at work, and someone else got it. Or, you thought you'd be married by now, but there are no prospects in sight. Maybe you have a sickness or infirmity that immobilizes you, or infertility prevents your dream of having your own family.

Each of these are disappointing circumstances, to say the least. It would be easy to think, "Why do these things always happen to me?" You look at others who appear less deserving, and marvel at how easily they glide forward. They plot out their lives, and circumstances quickly and simply line up for them. It just isn't fair.

You, of all people, understand the verse: *Hope deferred maketh the heart sick.* (Prov. 13:12a) That word *deferred* means "drawn out."

Unfulfilled expectations easily lead to thoughts of doom. You doubt that God cares, and you fear your life will always be like this. You can't get past "why?"

But the truth is that God has not disappeared. He is still over all, and He has His plans and purposes. It might encourage you to know that some of the most used-of-God people in the Bible had unfulfilled expectations.

Remember that the prophet Samuel anointed young David as king while Saul was still king. It was *years* before David actually became king, and before he did, he was forced by Saul into homelessness. When was this promise ever going to be fulfilled? It didn't look like it would ever happen. In fact, it looked like Saul was going to murder David before it *could* happen.

Consider the apostle Paul, the first great missionary, who had a crying need that he begged God to take care of. Remember that thorn in the flesh?

And lest I should be exalted above measure through the abundance of the revelations, there was given to me a thorn in the flesh, the messenger of Satan to buffet me, lest I should be exalted above measure. For this thing I besought the Lord thrice, that it might depart from me. And he said unto me, my grace is sufficient for thee: for my strength is made perfect in weakness. Most gladly therefore will I rather glory in my infirmities, that the power of Christ may rest upon me. Therefore I take pleasure in infirmities, in reproaches, in necessities, in persecutions, in distresses for Christ's sake: for when I am weak, then am I strong. (2 Cor. 12:7-10)

Paul may have felt like he was hindered from being all that he could be by this physical malady. He may have dreamed of how much more he could do, and perhaps he felt a little side-lined. But God doesn't think like we do. We know because Paul finally received the "why" of his circumstance. It was so that he wouldn't get too proud. It was a Satan-induced, God-prescribed infirmity to keep him humble. Hmm. Humility is more important to God than hyper service.

God knows what you would become if you received what you expect. He also knows what you can become if you don't receive what you want. Remember that God is the center of the universe, not you. His goal for you is not to be happy, healthy, fulfilled and comfortable. What God desires is His own glory and that His strength be made perfect in your weakness. Let God shine. Like John said, *He must increase, but I must decrease.* (John 3:30) Paul certainly got that. He got it so well, he was excited to have his physical ailment so God could become strong in his weakness.

Going deeper:

■ Read through Paul's account of his thorn in the flesh again in 2 Cor. 12 and ask God to show you what He wants you to learn. Ask Him to allow the lesson to stick and to help you through your challenges.

■ Memorize one of these verses:

—*For I know the thoughts that I think toward you, saith the LORD, thoughts of peace, and not of evil, to give you an expected end.* (Jer. 29:11)

—*My soul, wait thou only upon God; for my expectation is from him.* (Psa. 62:5)

Day 6: Doubt is Devilish

Doubt is one of the silent causes of depression for Christians. It seems like a small, harmless condition, but really, it's lethal. Why is that? Because doubt is a shield. Only instead of shielding against the enemy, it defends against God's grace.

Grace is only activated by faith. You know God can do anything, but He chooses not to when you doubt. You end up flailing around and eventually calling out to Him... more because you're in trouble than because you believe.

Remember when Peter saw Jesus walking on the water and had a sudden impulse to walk on water himself? Jesus encouraged him, and he jumped out of the boat and walked on water, until he looked around at the wind and waves and was afraid and started to sink. *And immediately Jesus stretched forth his hand, and caught him, and said unto him, O thou of little faith, wherefore didst thou doubt?* (Matt. 14:31)

Jesus had this to say about doubt in relation to faith: *Jesus answered and said unto them, Verily I say unto you, If ye have faith, and doubt not, ye shall not only do this which is done to the fig tree, but also if ye shall say unto this mountain, Be thou removed, and be thou cast into the sea; it shall be done.* (Matt. 21:21)

You may not be looking to move any mountains today. You would settle for a little peace and some hope. Fortunately, there's a remedy for doubt. It's faith. Believe God. Work on holding up that shield of faith to ward off the darts of the devil. By the way, Satan's darts are aimed at your mind. You may not realize it, but some of your negative self-talk is likely Satan whispering in your ear. And when it comes to spiritual things, he whispers, "God didn't really mean that." That's what he did to Eve. (Read Gen. 3:1-4.) He planted doubt in her mind about what God really said.

What if Eve would have held up the shield of faith—talked about in Eph. 6:16—and said, "Uh, let's look and see exactly what God said."? She wouldn't have sinned. Instead, she sent us all on the same path she took, doubting what God said and doubting that God meant what He said.

The key for you in getting over the malady of doubt is to find what God said that applies to your heart and your situation and believe it. Find a promise today before you go any further and pray it back to God. The Bible is full of promises. If you're in a hurry, maybe you can quickly hang on to the following verse: *But my God shall supply all your need according to his riches in glory by Christ Jesus.* (Phil. 4:19)

Going deeper:

■ Find your own promise from God in the Bible, ask Him to make it true on your behalf and tell Him you believe. Use these verses as your assurance that He will answer: *And this is the confidence that we have in him, that, if we ask any thing according to his will, he heareth us: And if we know that he hear us, whatsoever we ask, we know that we have the petitions that we desired of him.* (1 John 5:14-15)

■ On your own, study what the Bible has to say about doubt and its opposite—belief. Here are some verses to get you started: Luke 12:28-30; Mark 11:24; Eph. 1:17-20; 1 Thes. 2:13; Heb. 11:6. Write down the ones that are especially meaningful to you.

Day 7: Self-doubt is Sneaky

"I don't doubt God, I just doubt myself." Have you ever had that thought? God is great, but you're not sure you can live up to the expectations required to be right with Him. You know you'll fall, because you have so many times before. Down in the dumps you go.

In this case, fight failure with failure. By that I mean, don't think too highly of yourself. Reduce your self-expectations. *For I say, through the grace given unto me, to every man that is among you, not to think of himself more highly than he ought to think; but to think soberly.* (Rom. 12:3a)

Soberly means moderately. You're not that good, and you're not that bad. You are clay. Truly. You were taken from the dust, and to the dust you will go. But for the grace of God, that's about all.

The fact that you don't think too highly of your abilities to stay right with God is better than being proud of the abilities you do have. *Seest thou a man wise in his own conceit? There is more hope of a fool than of him.* (Prov. 26:12)

If nothing else, this book will teach you that being down on yourself is the first step in looking up to a great big God who loves to lift up people like you. *But he giveth more grace. Wherefore he saith, God resisteth the proud, but giveth grace unto the humble.* (James 4:6)

The difference is, you need to take your focus off your inabilities and instead turn your attention to God, who will catch you when you fall. He forgives. He moves on. Move on with Him by accepting and believing He forgave what you confessed and forsook. When you confess, He removes your sins as far away as the east is from west. (Ps. 103:12)

Resist the temptation to go deep within yourself to "figure yourself out." *A fool hath no delight in understanding, but that his heart may discover itself.* (Prov. 18:2) Contrary to pop-psychology, excessive self-analysis can hinder your emotional/spiritual growth by leading you to blame your feelings and circumstances on your upbringing. You open yourself up to self-pity for your regretful past and assume that you are doomed to a life of failure as a result.

What you need to know is, yes, you will likely fail. You may have already fallen greatly. The question is, have you asked for forgiveness and repented from whatever it was you did? If so, you are forgiven. There's no need to keep beating yourself up over what God has already forgiven. His forgiveness is complete. He doesn't bring it back up again.

Even the apostle Paul grappled with self-doubt. He knew the right thing to do, but he found something inside that didn't want to do it. Instead, he found himself doing the very thing he knew was wrong. That bugged him. (Read Rom. 7)

Here's Paul's conclusion about his failings: *There is therefore now no condemnation to them which are in Christ Jesus, who walk not after the flesh, but after the Spirit. For the law of the Spirit of life in Christ Jesus hath made me free from the law of sin and death.* (Rom. 8:1-2)

You might be tempted to rally yourself and do great things for God to prove to yourself that you're worthy of God's grace. All that "doing" amounts to self-exercise. You may never have thought of this next verse in that light, but read this: *For bodily exercise profiteth little: but godliness is profitable unto all things, having promise of the life that now is, and of that which is to come.* (1 Tim. 4:7b-8) The only work you need to do is work on your communication with God. Start listening to Him in His word, and start talking to Him in prayer. Get close to Him and godliness will come, not from exercising yourself, but from quietly abiding in Him. *I am the vine, ye are the branches: He that abideth in me, and I in him, the same bringeth forth much fruit: for without me ye can do nothing.* (John 15:5)

Going deeper:

Learn to think soberly about yourself, meaning don't think too highly or too lowly of yourself. Jesus died for you, which shows how valuable you are to Him. But He died for everyone else too. Somewhere in the middle is the balance. You really aren't any more special to God than anyone else. With that in mind, meditate on these verses: Phil. 2:3-8; Rom. 12:10; Eph. 4:7&17.

Day 8: Guilt is No Trip

If you're like me, when you go on a trip, you have to find a keepsake to bring back to keep the good memories. In my case, I collect turtles. I have a little table that's like a time capsule of most of my trips. It holds turtles and memories from everywhere... Singapore, Hawaii, Chile, Springfield, Mo., India, California, etc.

But there's one trip you don't want to go on, and if you do, you don't want souvenirs: a guilt trip. You don't want a regular remembrance of what you've done, because it causes anxiety, feelings of unworthiness, imaginations of being forsaken by God and others, unrelenting disappointment in yourself, ongoing shame and more. If you don't learn what to do with that heavy load, you'll go under for days, and maybe weeks to a lifetime.

Maybe you bear the physical or emotional scars from a choice you made years ago that prevents you from forgetting what you did, and you're tormented by the memories and the turmoil. You've asked yourself if God can forgive, and even though you know mentally that He did forgive you when you asked, you feel like you don't deserve any more special favors from God. You haven't forgiven yourself, and deep down, you don't truly believe that God has either. You imagine it comes up in God's mind as it does in your mind.

If that's the cause of your despair, there is hope. But it will require reprogramming your mind. It will also require taking yourself in hand, and rather than listening to yourself, you will need to begin talking to yourself. It will be a process at first, but eventually, you will be delivered.

First, the sin you think is unforgiveable is only a blip on God's radar. Think of the worst thing you could do. I think that would be murder. Could God forgive and use someone who has murdered someone else?

Consider Moses. *And he looked this way and that way, and when he saw that there was no man, he slew the Egyptian, and hid him in the sand.* (Ex. 2:12) He murdered someone. Even that did not disqualify him from a life filled with God's close presence. It was after this event that God called Moses from the burning bush and made him a leader. It was after this event when Moses was called God's friend. *And there arose not a prophet since in Israel like unto Moses, whom the LORD knew face to face.* (Deut. 34:10) You may not have problems believing that God would respond to someone else that way, but you must believe that it's true for you too.

It may even have been that very murder that made Moses a meek man. *Now the man Moses was very meek, above all the men which were upon the face of the earth.* (Num. 12:3) The word *meek* means poor, weak and afflicted. I'm sure the memory of his murder never left his mind. But rather than disqualify him, it put him in a condition in which God could use him, because God gives grace to the humble, contrite person.

19

If you can just look upward rather than look inward, you will find grace, favor and even peace—maybe for the first time. *Who is among you that feareth the LORD, that obeyeth the voice of his servant, that walketh in darkness, and hath no light? let him trust in the name of the LORD, and stay upon his God.* (Isa. 50:10) *Thou wilt keep him in perfect peace, whose mind is stayed on thee: because he trusteth in thee.* (Isa. 26:3)

Trusting God is a process, just like building a new friendship. You don't trust someone you don't know well until that person proves trustworthy. As you see that God is trustworthy, and that He still answers prayer and provides blessings aplenty, in spite of you, you will grow in trust. Eventually, you will leave the guilt behind.

Going deeper:

■ If guilt is one of your main causes of depression, here is an exercise for you. Take out a piece of paper and write down the things you have done for which you feel guilty. Have you confessed them to God before? If not, now is the time. If you have, write your feelings about the guilt you still hold onto, including whatever doubts and fears that have arisen because of what you have done. Truly. Spend some time on this. Next, read 1 John 1:9 and thank Him for His forgiveness. Then take a magic marker and write "1 John 1:9" across the page. Tell God you trust that He forgave you. Then wad up that paper and throw it away. It's gone. It's time for a fresh start. Finally, determine before God not to go back to the actions and habits that you just confessed. Read Proverbs 28:13.

■ Other Bible characters besides Moses made bad choices that could have left them mired in guilty unworthiness. Meditate on Paul's (Saul's) unworthy actions of participating in the stoning of Stephen (Acts 7:54-60) and how God called and used him anyway. Ponder the prophet Jonah's stinky attitude regarding God's request that he warn the Ninevites to repent (Johan 4:1-3). God still used Jonah, who finally obeyed, though Jonah never did adjust his attitude to align with God.

Day 9: Capture Your Wild Imagination

Your imagination has the potential to jerk you around from the moment you wake up in the morning to the time you fall asleep at night. The thoughts of your mind take you on a trip every day, in fact many trips, including guilt trips and to pity parties and doubt fests. Your mind with its imaginations can drive you to fits of anger and jealousy and then stop you cold with fear. You work yourself into a lather over something that hasn't even happened. You just imagine that it could.

There is no limit to the places you can go each day. Truth be told, your mind probably takes you down the same path every day with only a few side excursions. It's possible you're in a thought rut. You might be more prone to wandering along with low-grade anger and suspicion or doubt and fear.

Don't let those imaginations take the steering wheel and accelerator of your day. Learn to use your brake pedal and catch yourself before you turn down the path of feeling sorry for yourself, doubting God, and thinking everyone should fall in step with your ideas and plans. In fact, stop for a minute. What does God say?

Over and over He tells us to be sober with our minds. That means self-controlled and temperate. Take yourself in hand and direct your thoughts rather than listen to your thoughts. You may have heard the old phrase "an idle mind is the devil's workshop." It's not in the Bible, but it is certainly true. Unless you consciously control your thoughts, Satan will be there with his suggestions. *Be sober, be vigilant; because your adversary the devil, as a roaring lion, walketh about, seeking whom he may devour: Whom resist stedfast in the faith.* (1 Pet. 5:8-9a)

How do you resist the devil and the thoughts he hurls at you? Learn to make a habit of 2 Cor. 10:5: *Casting down imaginations, and every high thing that exalteth itself against the knowledge of God, and bringing into captivity every thought to the obedience of Christ.*

That is a key to preventing depression. You just don't allow yourself to dwell on the random thoughts that rise up all day. Neither do you succumb to the ideals of friends, television, reading material or anything else. Instead, you replace murky views with true thoughts. (The list of approved thoughts is in Phil. 4:8.) The best place to find true thoughts is the Bible, of course. Its truths are not stagnant. The Bible isn't passively true. *For the word of God is quick, and powerful, and sharper than any two-edged sword, piercing even to the dividing asunder of soul and spirit, and of the joints and marrow, and is a discerner of the thoughts and intents of the heart.* (Heb. 4:12)

So shall my word be that goeth forth out of my mouth: it shall not return unto me void, but it shall accomplish that which I please, and it shall prosper in the thing whereto I sent it. (Isa. 55:11)

Is not my word like as a fire? saith the LORD; and like a hammer that breaketh the rock in pieces? (Jer. 23:29)

The Bible is the place to go for a transformed mind. That means memorizing and meditating on the verses that address your challenging thoughts and attitudes, some of which you have identified over the past eight days.

Going deeper:

I applied a form of what I'm about to suggest in 1983 when the book "Do You Hear What You're Thinking?" was released. Author Jerry Schmidt suggested identifying the thoughts that plague you and writing "counter cards." That is, for each index card, write a reoccurring ugly thought that frequently infects you. On the reverse side of each card, write Bible verses that counter that thought. Keep the cards handy, and when one of those ugly thoughts pops into your head, read the back of the card. I did it and was amazed at how it changed my mental and emotional constitution over time. Those common bad thoughts disappeared, and in their place came a sense of well-being.

Why did that work? Because my besetting troubled thoughts are not so much psychological as they are spiritual. So to fight them, I needed something spiritual—the Word of God—which happens to also be the only offensive weapon given to us to fight our spiritual mind battles. (*And take the helmet of salvation, and the sword of the Spirit, which is the word of God.* Eph. 6:17) Keep in mind, this is the Word of God, not just the thoughts of God. So get to know His very words.

Assignment

Throughout the remainder of this book, we are going to do something similar to counter cards. We will call it the ABCs of Spiritual Health.

For each letter of the alphabet, find a verse that will help with your mental/emotional/spiritual well-being. Write these verses either on 3- by 5-inch cards or start a computer file called ABCs of Spiritual Health and record them there. The particular verse for each letter of the alphabet doesn't have to start with the letter, just the key word in the verse that will help you to remember it.

Finish the alphabet and review your verses often, especially when you are down.

I will remind you and offer verse suggestions throughout the rest of this book. It's an assignment you will not forget, because I won't let you. From here on, you will find links to verse YouTube videos and verse pictures on my blog site, mastertruth.com. Keep in mind, though, that the verses on your list are yours. The verses I share are just suggestions.

I'm not asking you to do something I haven't already done—twice. More than 15 years ago, I was assigned the task of coming up with a personal list of ABC verses for a happy marriage. It has been a life-saver. I also have an ABC verse list to combat depression. Your ABC verses for Spiritual Health will be your life-savers. There are 26 letters in the alphabet, and you have 22 days left in this devotional. Hopefully, by the end, you will have your own list of verses to help you cope and control your thoughts so that you get out and stay out of depression.

Here is the first suggested verse. It goes with the letter "C" for "casting" or "I" for "imagination." *Casting down imaginations, and every high thing that exalteth itself against the knowledge of God, and bringing into captivity every thought to the obedience of Christ*; (2 Cor. 10:5) To help you learn 2 Cor. 10:3&5, look for the verse reference on YouTube under Jody Shee. You can also find a colorful, printable 5- by 7-inch photo on mastertruth.com. Click on the "Free photos" tab on the right and search for "imaginations" for the link to download the photo.

PART 2: INNER POSTURE

Depression is an inner lowness. Remember Webster's dictionary definition of depressed? It means "pressed or forced down; lowed; sunk; dejected; dispirited; sad; humbled."

Some parts of that definition don't sound that bad. In fact, God would rather that you be humbled than that you be lifted up. Stay with me through this seven-day section, and you will get a firm hold on what God has to say about a "lowed" condition. As I mentioned earlier, depression in some form is widely discussed in the Bible. You won't find the word *depressed*, but you'll find many angles and hues of the concept. Be encouraged. Down moments (and even days of it) give God something to work with.

I promise, by the time you are done with this section, you will be happy that you are sad, which reminds me of a profound quote I memorized years ago that I believe is from D. Martyn Lloyd-Jones: *A mature disciplined Christian has learned to feel just as good when he feels bad as he does when he feels good.* The loftiness of that statement intrigues and challenges me.

As you learn about inner posture and disciplines, realize that part of what you are dealing with may be your personality type. Introverts have a greater tendency to introspection and depression. It's just the way God made some people. This section will teach you how to reap positive benefits from this type of disposition that jovial extroverts may never comprehend.

Day 10: Sparky People

Is self-ambition OK? Or is that even a question that should be asked? During the three months I spent as a summer missionary in England years ago, I had a conversation about self-ambition with a guy at one of the churches I was helping. He felt compelled to explain that he thought American Christians are too ambitious, and God doesn't like that. We're always planning what we are going to do and how we are going to do it. We should depend and wait on the Lord. Radical. That's what I thought about him.

If I didn't have self-ambition, I don't think I could get out of bed in the morning. But in one sense I see his point— every now and then. Because most of the time, I'm thinking and planning and dreaming and doing.

But read these verses with me and think about them in the context of self-ambition: *Who is among you that feareth the LORD, that obeyeth the voice of his servant, that walketh in darkness, and hath no light? Let him trust in the name of the LORD, and stay upon his God. Behold, all ye that kindle a fire, that compass yourselves about with sparks: walk in the light of your fire, and in the sparks that ye have kindled. This shall ye have of mine hand; ye shall lie down in sorrow.* (Isa. 50:10-11)

Wow! Do you see what I see in those verses? God is talking about what I have come to call *sparky people.* They make stuff happen, and here, it's not a good thing. That's because in this context, sparky people are cutting their own path, making their own mark, finding their own solutions—apart from God. It reminds me of this verse: *Some trust in chariots, and some in horses: but we will remember the name of the LORD our God.* (Psa. 20:7) The sparks kindled by those who are self-ambitious will die out. It's impossible for the fire of self-reliance to burn steadily.

Those who don't know the Lord, of course are all about self-ambition, because God's will and God's path aren't even in their thoughts. But many who don't know the Lord accomplish great things through their ambition. Some develop drugs to cure cancer. Some find solutions to problems through technology. Some engineer great inventions. What they dream and do can be magnificent. So, is there anything wrong with that?

To that, I would say that God gave some people tremendous talents and abilities to accomplish wonderful things, but not in a vacuum. Remember that in Him we live and move and have our being. (Acts 17:28) And to the Israelites in Deuteronomy, He said: *Who fed thee in the wilderness with manna, which thy fathers knew not, that he might humble thee, and that he might prove thee, to do thee good at thy latter end; And thou say in thine heart, My power and the might of mine hand hath gotten me this wealth. But thou shalt remember the LORD thy God: for it is he that giveth thee power to get wealth...* (Deut. 8:17-18a)

The Israelites demonstrated what happens when we go off on our own trails. Sometimes I do that too. I readily ride off on my own ideas and don't consult God.

Here's God's wisdom on that. *For thus saith the Lord GOD, the Holy One of Israel; In returning and rest shall ye be saved; in quietness and in confidence shall be your strength: and ye would not. But ye said, No; for we will flee upon horses; therefore shall ye flee: and, we will ride upon the swift; therefore shall they that pursue you be swift.* (Isa. 30:15-16)

The lesson is to humble yourself before God. Submit to His will. Acknowledge Him and He will direct your paths. (Prov. 3:5-6)

The closing point I want to make is that often, those who feel depressed and lowly often lack self-ambition completely—to even clean themselves and their space, to take care of daily matters, maybe to even get out of bed. If that describes you, develop some disciplines. Determine to accomplish something, and call a friend to be accountable to function normally. God is not down on you, but He also doesn't want you to succumb to despair. Ask for His help to rise up. He will answer you.

Going deeper:

Remember, it's better to be still before the Lord than to kindle a fire and live in your sparks. Today, work on your ABCs of Spiritual Health list. Is there a verse in this lesson you could use on your list? Remember, it's the key word in the verse that determines what letter of the alphabet to put it under. Consider this verse for "Q:" *For thus saith the Lord GOD, the Holy One of Israel; In returning and rest shall ye be saved; in quietness and in confidence shall be your strength.* (Isa. 30:15a) You can find a scenic, printable 5- by 7-inch photo with this verse on mastertruth.com. Click on the "Free photos" tab on the right and search for "quietness" for the link to download the photo.

Day 11: Silver Goblets

Can we all agree that we, as Christians, are vessels for the Master's use? Some of us are delicate fine china; some are handy Dixie cups; some are durable Tupperware cups. I would like to address you silver goblets out there. These vessels can be used ceremoniously, but they also have a practical place in the Kingdom of God. I'm calling a meek person (who is bankrupt in spirit and emotionally needy, and not just in a biblical sense) a silver goblet. Work with me here.

My dad used to own a brass foundry. Part of his business involved making objects from metals. With huge furnaces and big round pots, he melted metal scraps and poured the red-hot liquid into molds. On the top of the red melted liquid, scum would form. It had to be skimmed off. It was the product waste, or dross. If you ever go to a foundry and watch the process, know that God is watching it with you and has a lesson: *Take away the dross from the silver, and there shall come forth a vessel for the finer.* (Prov. 25:4)

Back to our silver goblets—and you might be one yourself—of melancholy nature, frequently down in the dumps, unable to rise up. That "down in the dumps" or severe sense of self-inadequacy, is the dross that needs to be skimmed off from a perfectly useful silver cup in the Father's hands.

You're not useless, as you might feel you sometimes are. In fact, your self-deprecation, if submitted to God, puts you right where He can use you.

Moses was like that. When God appeared to him from the burning bush in Exodus 3 and explained how He, God, was going to use Moses to lead the Israelites out of Egypt, Moses' response wasn't, "Wow, I can hardly wait." It was, *I am not eloquent... but I am slow of speech, and of a slow tongue.* (Ex. 4:10) Moses did not think highly of himself. Even after God explained further that He made Moses like that, Moses still wallowed a bit in self-inadequacy. But we know the rest of the story, and God did use him, and God often spoke with Moses as to a friend (Ex. 33:11).

What was it about Moses that God really liked? It was his meekness. *Now the man Moses was very meek, above all the men which were upon the face of the earth.* (Num. 12:3) It means poor, humble and needy. It's not necessarily a holy-child-of-God characteristic. It's just that people who are meek in the sense of "needy" will turn to God for strength. They will depend on Him. Remember to cast your cares on the Lord right away. Rather than get on the phone and cry to your friends and family, call out to God. Let Him be your first choice for comfort and encouragement.

Jesus was also meek: *Take my yoke upon you, and learn of me; for I am meek and lowly in heart: and ye shall find rest unto your souls.* (Matt. 11:29) He asks us to be meek, too. *Put on therefore, as the elect of God, holy and beloved, bowels of mercies, kindness, humbleness of mind, meekness, longsuffering.* (Col. 3:12)

For some people—our silver goblets—being meek, or of low spirit, is just who they are. And maybe that's you. You're not flamboyant or the life of the party. You are more inward, and you brood easily. You are introspective and easily see faults in yourself and others. Amidst all of that, there is some dross that needs to be skimmed off. Don't let the negative thoughts overpower you and render you useless. Say, "Yes God. Whatever you want me to do, even though I don't feel adequate, I'll do it." Then find your strength in this promise: *For it is God which worked in you both to will <u>and to do</u> of his good pleasure.* (Phil. 2:13) Give God some credit right now for sustaining your will and your ability to walk with Him.

Going deeper:

■ Meditate on this verse written by Paul: *Therefore I take pleasure in infirmities, in reproaches, in necessities, in persecutions, in distresses for Christ's sake: for when I am weak, then am I strong.* (2 Cor. 12:10)

—Thinking of this verse, list all your "infirmities." This could be personality characteristics you don't especially like in yourself or limitations placed on you by people or circumstances outside your control. Ask yourself if God knows about all those things and if they are too confining for Him to work with.

—Whatever limitations you list, stop and thank God for them. Then realize that those are the parameters you have to work within. Ask God to use you within those parameters.

■ Work on your ABCs for Spiritual Health list with "M" for meek. There are several you might choose from to add to your list and to memorize:

The meek also shall increase their joy in the LORD, and the poor among men shall rejoice in the Holy One of Israel. (Isa. 29:19)

The LORD lifteth up the meek. (Psa. 147:6a) You can find a colorful, printable 5- by 7-inch photo on mastertruth.com. Click on the "Free photos" tab on the right and search for "meek" for the link to download the photo.

■ About that idea of feeling useless that needs to be tweaked. You may have self-talk going on in your head in which you condemn your life and your inabilities. If you have a reoccurring thought like that, write it on the front of a 3-inch by 5-inch card. On the back, write some verses you know that indicate you aren't useless. Whenever your reoccurring depressing thought pops into your head, find your card and read the verses you wrote on the back. This will reprogram your mind. Eventually, that ugly thought won't plague you anymore.

Day 12: Contrite is OK

Some people feel, speak and move around uninhibited and have a lot of friends. Do you ever envy them and feel emotionally lame in comparison? I do.

Remember in the Bible, after David's best friend Jonathan was killed in battle, David went looking for any family member of Jonathan's that he could find in order to show kindness to him. (If you're not familiar with the reason why he did it, read 1 Sam. 20:11-15.) While searching for a family member, David discovered that Jonathan had a son named Mephibosheth who was "lame in both feet." David asked someone to go fetch Mephibosheth, and feeling fearful and trembling, the poor guy was brought to David. *And David said unto him, Fear not: for I will surely shew thee kindness for Jonathan thy father's sake, and will restore thee all the land of Saul thy father; and thou shalt eat bread at my table continually.* (2 Sam. 9:7) Through no mustering of his own genius, Mephibosheth got to live off of the king's favor from then on.

You know what's interesting? That term *lame* that is used to describe Mephibosheth is translated *contrite* in other places.

David is a type of Jesus Christ in many ways. And here he showed kindness and favor to a contrite person. Contrite means crushed, collapsed, broken, dust. That pretty much describes Mephibosheth, and maybe it describes you sometimes. But now read what God thinks of crushed, collapsed, broken people who feel like dust:

The LORD is nigh unto them that are of a broken heart; and saveth such as be of a contrite spirit. (Psa. 34:18)

The sacrifices of God are a broken spirit: a broken and a contrite heart, O God, thou wilt not despise. (Psa. 51:17)

For thus saith the high and lofty One that inhabiteth eternity, whose name is Holy; I dwell in the high and holy place, with him also that is of a contrite and humble spirit, to revive the spirit of the humble, and to revive the heart of the contrite ones. (Isa. 57:15)

For all those things hath mine hand made, and all those things have been, saith the LORD: but to this man will I look, even to him that is poor and of a contrite spirit, and trembleth at my word. (Isa. 66:2)

Just like David, God looks for someone to show kindness to, and wouldn't you know, He chooses the same kind of person David chose: contrite, broken, humble and crushed. He gives grace to the humble, help to the weak. He lifts up the broken hearted and comes to the aid of the meek.

If you are prone to depression, those verses would be good ones to print out on a card and hang around the house. God is *for* you. Everyone should be contrite so they can experience God's attention, presence and reviving.

Here, pray David's prayer: *I am feeble and sore broken: I have roared by reason of the disquietness of my heart.*

(Psa. 38:8) *Sore broken* means contrite. Call out to God. He is listening and ready to come alongside and revive you.

Going deeper:

■ From the group of four verses above (Psa. 34:18; 51:17; Isa. 57:15; 66:2), compile a list of positives, or benefits, of being contrite that you observe.

■ As you work on your ABCs for Spiritual Health verse list, you need a "C" word. Contrite would be a great one. Perhaps a verse from today's lesson jumps out at you. Here is my favorite: *For all those things hath mine hand made, and all those things have been, saith the LORD: but to this man will I look, even to him that is poor and of a <u>contrite</u> spirit, and trembleth at my word.* (Isa. 66:2) You will find a colorful, printable 5- by 7-inch photo on mastertruth.com. Go to the "Free photos" tab on the right and search for "contrite" for the link to download the photo.

Day 13: Get a Little Lower

When God looks down from heaven, you know the person He is particularly looking for? It's the humble person. This is the person He exalts. If you generally feel down, you are close to the right position before God.

The problem is, when you feel crushed, weak and emotionally helpless, the tendency is to focus inward rather than call out to God. If that's you, remember you are a silver goblet in the making, and the dross that needs to be skimmed off is that tendency to writhe in emotional anguish with no thought of God. He's right there with you. Call out to Him.

How do you become humble, by the way? *Humble* means to lower yourself. It shows on the outside as submitting to God and to others. Humility works on the inside. Submission shows on the outside. You might be humble in heart, but to submit, there's someone outside you that you are lowering yourself before. Consider this:

Likewise, ye younger, submit yourselves unto the elder. Yea, all of you be subject one to another, and be clothed with humility: for God resisteth the proud, and giveth grace to the humble. Humble yourselves therefore under the mighty hand of God, that he may exalt you in due time. (1 Pet. 5:5-6)

Let others be more important than you. Let them go first. Put yourself last. I know, it's not natural. Submission isn't a quality you pray for. It's something you willingly, consciously do. Look at the verbs in the above verses. Submit yourselves… be subject one to another… be clothed with humility… Humble yourselves.

The best example I can think of is Jesus—God in the flesh. He came from the most exalted position to live among us. And He didn't come to be ministered to, but to minister (Mark 10:45). He humbled Himself and became obedient to the point of death (Phil. 2:8). He came from as high as you can come to go as low as you can go. And He did it consciously… willingly. Just how was He able to do that? Here's how: *Who, when he was reviled, reviled not again; when he suffered, he threatened not; but committed himself to him that judgeth righteously.* (1 Pet. 2:23) He didn't stand up for Himself. He didn't say, "Hey, do you know who my Father is?" He said nothing. Instead, He put Himself in God's hands. And that's what you do when you submit to God and humble yourself. You commit yourself to God, not just once in your life, but daily. Maybe hourly.

So, here's the point for today. When you feel crushed, weak, beaten down and emotionally helpless, submit to God. *For we have not an high priest which cannot be touched with the feeling of our infirmities; but was in all points tempted like as we are, yet without sin. Let us therefore come boldly unto the throne of grace, that we may obtain mercy, and find grace to help in time of need.* (Heb. 4:15-16)

To look around is to be distressed. To look within is to be depressed. To look up is to be blessed.

Going deeper:

■ It's time to submit or surrender everything to God, even the things you didn't realize you needed to surrender. Instead of praying and saying, "I surrender everything to you, God," get out a piece of paper or start a *surrender* file on your computer. Make a list of things you may never have specifically mentioned to God. These could be things that you consider to be physical, mental, emotional, situational or spiritual deficits in your life. Your list could look something like this: lack of money, few friends, no talents, a huge nose, easily angry, no energy, etc.

■ The list might look pretty depressing when you're done with it. But don't stop there. Now pray through each thing you wrote down and give it to God. While he knows everything on that list already, He wants to know you aren't going to hang on to them by yourself. Express how they make you feel, but then give them over to Him. Give Him permission to have them and ask for His grace to handle them. Tell Him you will bear them for His glory, if He wants. Just deal with each one in the presence of God.

Day 14: Humility with Benefits

The idea of being humble might sound good, if you're a hermit. But you might live a highly visible life, interacting with people at work and socially. Perhaps you're a leader at church. If you go around acting humble and meek, you'll get stomped on as others in your sphere pass you up. There are some pretty strong personalities out there who will gladly kick you out of the way on their way up.

The world will teach you how to be assertive, if not by seminar, at least by example. I once had a pretty low-level job and minded my own business when a gal made it known that she wanted pieces of my job. I, not being one to readily stand up for myself, wrung my hands and lost sleep over the idea that she might actually find ways to take away the fun parts of my job.

By personality, you might not be the type to stand up for yourself, so you think you're doomed to live at the bottom of opportunity. Once again, you find yourself alone in the abyss, envying those with stronger personalities who know how to get what they want.

But here's a secret. The benefit of being humble, meek and entrusting yourself to God is that He lifts you up. You don't do it yourself, He does it. Let me show you:

For whosoever exalteth himself shall be abased; and he that humbleth himself shall be exalted. (Luke 14:11)

A man's pride shall bring him low: but honour shall uphold the humble in spirit. (Prov. 29:23)

When men are cast down, then thou shalt say, There is lifting up; and he shall save the humble person. (Job 22:29)

Remember, God doesn't think like we think. His ways aren't our ways, and His thoughts aren't our thoughts. Yes, the world says to claw and fight your way into prominence, but God says to lower yourself a few notches and let Him lift you up. This next passage is profound, and you may see things in it you have never seen. Read carefully, and maybe twice. Don't miss it:

But he giveth more grace. Wherefore he saith, God resisteth the proud, but giveth grace unto the humble. Submit yourselves therefore to God. Resist the devil, and he will flee from you. Draw nigh to God, and he will draw nigh to you. Cleanse your hands, ye sinners; and purify your hearts, ye double minded. <u>Be afflicted, and mourn, and weep: let your laughter be turned to mourning, and your joy to heaviness.</u> Humble yourselves in the sight of the Lord, and he shall lift you up. (James 4:6-10)

Doesn't it sound a little like God is telling you to be depressed in order to humble yourself so He can lift you up? (Look back at Day 10: Sparky People.) He says to be afflicted. That means to feel miserable. He says to turn your joy to heaviness. That means dejection and gloom. Hmm. You might feel like you're already there. So look at the benefit of that if you will turn your focus to Him. Praise

35

Him. Say, "Thank you Jesus. Please lift me up right now, because I have no strength in myself." It will be easier for Him to lift you up if you will at least look up! Don't let affliction turn into depression. After all, we are promised affliction (see 2 Cor. 4:17-18 for encouragement).

You don't have to look around at others. You don't have to look inside at what a wretch you feel like. Just look up and take hold of God. He will lift you up! Then you're better off than those stronger personalities who lift themselves up.

Going deeper:

■ Personalize the following verses by reading them a few times first, then talk to God about them in whatever way you are impressed to pray: *The lofty looks of man shall be humbled, and the haughtiness of men shall be bowed down, and the LORD alone shall be exalted in that day. For the day of the LORD of hosts shall be upon every one that is proud and lofty, and upon every one that is lifted up; and he shall be brought low.* (Isa. 2:11-12)

■ Are you working on your ABC verses for Spiritual Health? There are several terrific ones in this lesson. Your "H" word could be humble, or it could be honor, as in God honoring the humble person. *A man's pride shall bring him low: but honour shall uphold the humble in spirit.* (Prov. 29:23) For a colorful, printable 5- by 7-inch photo of this verse, go to mastertruth.com to the "Free photos" tab on the right and search for "honor" for the link to download the photo.

Day 15: Pliable People

By now you've seen that the kind of heart God can work with is the lowly and humble heart. We'll call those the pliable people. God loves them. He expects people to be pliable in His hands, and it only comes with humility and submission to Him.

A humble heart is one that is closer to the earth…a little more desperate and needy. I know, it's not the way we think we should live. We think we should step out the door in the morning ready to conquer. But those who are self-sufficient and self-relying don't need or acknowledge God. As I've said before, our parents raised us to be independent, but God is raising us to be dependent, on Him. And so we're back to the humble heart.

Often the first time a word is mentioned in the Bible sets the tone for its meaning throughout the Bible. The first time *humble* appears, it's a message for the wicked Pharaoh who is holding the Israelites captive in Egypt, refusing to let them go and making their lives miserable. God chooses His spokesmen, Moses and Aaron: *And Moses and Aaron came in unto Pharaoh, and said unto him, Thus saith the LORD God of the Hebrews, How long wilt thou refuse to humble thyself before me? Let my people go, that they may serve me.* (Ex. 10:3)

Lack of humbleness before God was Pharaoh's issue. It means *afflict* and *oppress*. And all through the Bible, God wants people to be humble before Him. It only happens when we're brought low, crushed and needy, as we've already seen. Why does He want us humble? So we'll be obedient to Him. Pharaoh wasn't obedient in letting God's people go because he wasn't humble. Pride refuses God's will. Humility says, "Yes God."

The humble/obedience connection is underscored the next time the word *humble* appears in the Bible. It's in Deuteronomy, and it's after the Israelites have been freed from Egypt, but are wandering in the wilderness for 40 years. *And thou shalt remember all the way which the LORD thy God led thee these forty years in the wilderness, to humble thee, and to prove thee, to know what was in thine heart, whether thou wouldest keep his commandments, or no.* (Deut. 8:2)

Why did the Israelites have to wander in the wilderness for 40 years? To humble them. To prove what was in their heart. To see if they would obey God. Why do you have to go through whatever difficulty you do? If it's not the result of sin and bad choices you have made, it could be that it's part of God's examination process to test your obedience.

If the idea of being humble is just about afflicting us, that's a little hard to understand. But look at the third time the word is used, also in the context of the Israelites wandering around in the wilderness for 40 years. *Who fed thee in the wilderness with manna, which thy fathers knew not, that he might humble thee, and that he might prove thee, to do thee good at thy latter end.* (Deut. 8:16) The result of us humbling ourselves is so God can show us His goodness. If we're obedient, humble children of God, He can work with us in goodness rather than in discipline.

The New Testament supports God's ultimate goodness resulting from our humility. *Humble yourselves therefore under the mighty hand of God, that he may exalt you in due time:* (1 Pet. 5:6)

So, if you are being crushed, afflicted and oppressed, ask God what He wants to teach you and how you can grow through this. Tell Him you know this isn't for naught. Submit to whatever it is He has for you. He is looking for obedience, so make sure you do whatever you know for sure He wants you to do. If there's a sin to confess and forsake, take care of it today.

He that covereth his sins shall not prosper: but whoso confesseth and forsaketh them shall have mercy. (Prov. 28:13)

Going deeper:

God sends tests and trials to prove us. What is He trying to prove? Several things. Make note of the reasons you observe from these verses: Deut. 8:2; 13:3; Gen. 22:11&12; Ex. 16:4; 2 Chron. 32:31. Is there some way He is testing and proving you right now? Are you passing?

Day 16: Meekness Looks Ahead

D id God ever use anyone greatly in the Bible who was poor in spirit and emotionally needy? If you think about it for a few minutes, you'll think of several people. Some, who were usually valiant, had spells of neediness. David did many times. Elijah found himself under a tree wishing to die. Jonah also had his struggles. These were great people with moments of meekness.

As we've already observed, Moses was emotionally needy, and God used him greatly.

Jesus was meek too. *Take my yoke upon you, and learn of me; for I am meek and lowly in heart: and ye shall find rest unto your souls.* (Matt. 11:29) Meek for Him meant he was gentle and mild. But He was also lowly in heart. *Lowly* in Greek means brought low with grief, depressed.

What? Jesus was depressed? He was God, and He was depressed. If you consider all He went through, you know why. His point in mentioning it is in verse 28. *Come unto me, all ye that labour and are heavy laden, and I will give you rest.* He identifies with you. He had low points in His life. But He made it through. We have the advantage, because we can see His life, beginning to end, and we know the purpose for His suffering. In our own lives, we only see right now, and we don't see the purpose.

How did Jesus make it through His depressing times? He looked ahead. He thought past what He was going through. He knew the future looked better. *Looking unto Jesus the author and finisher of our faith; who for the joy that was set before him endured the cross, despising the shame, and is set down at the right hand of the throne of God.* (Heb. 12:2)

Looking ahead was also how Paul made it through his trials and how he instructed us to make it through ours. *For our light affliction, which is but for a moment, worketh for us a far more exceeding and eternal weight of glory; While we look not at the things which are seen, but at the things which are not seen: for the things which are seen are temporal; but the things which are not seen are eternal.* (2 Cor. 4:17-18)

Can you do that? Can you look down the pike and see better days through spiritual eyes? Until your faith becomes sight in the presence of the Lord, capture this: *For we have not an high priest which cannot be touched with the feeling of our infirmities; but was in all points tempted like as we are, yet without sin. Let us therefore come boldly unto the throne of grace, that we may obtain mercy, and find grace to help in time of need.* (Heb. 4:15-16)

If looking forward doesn't help, look up. You're in good company. Jesus understands, and He has the power to help you.

And being found in fashion as a man, he humbled himself, and became obedient unto death, even the death of the cross. (Phil. 2:8) He made it through the worst thing that can happen to a person. Put yourself, your emotions and your circumstances in His hands. He can help you make it through your hard times.

Going deeper:

■ I've suggested to "look up" several times through this book so far. Perhaps that advice is starting to sound hollow. It's time to meditate on some verses that tell us where to place our focus. Examine these verses and write your impressions: Isa. 8:17; 31:1; 45:22; Micah 7:7; Titus 2:12-13; Jude 1:21

■ If you're experiencing times of lowness, you may have realized for the first time today that you are in good company, because Jesus was also low. Join up with Him and decide it's OK to be lowly together. If you're working on your ABC verses for Spiritual Health, your "Y" verse could be this one for "yolk." *Take my yoke upon you, and learn of me; for I am meek and lowly in heart: and ye shall find rest unto your souls.* (Matt. 11:29) To help you memorize this verse, print out the 5- by 7-inch photo from mastertruth.com. Go to the "Free photos" tab on the right and search for "yoke." There's a link to download the photo.

PART 3: LOVINGKINDNESS RULES

Hopefully this far into our topic of depression, you've found a few ideas and verses that you can hang on to. Maybe your perspective has already begun to change here and there. Now you're in for a treat. So far we've looked at ourselves and what God has to say about our maladies and dispositions. Now let's take the spotlight off of ourselves and on to God and one delightful, true characteristic of His that will change your life. That is, He is the God of lovingkindnesses.

I've been a connoisseur of this concept for 30 years. When I discovered from the Bible and from my life that He delights in showing unreserved, undeserved lovingkindnesses, I started keeping a notebook of some amazing lovingkindnesses He has shown me. The purpose of the notebook is to remind me how awesome God is so I don't get lost in my own introspective world and so I can share and encourage others with it.

Let's spend some time on the topic. First, let me offer a definition: Lovingkindnesses are the special little unexpected things God does for us because He loves us, even though we don't deserve them and sometimes don't even think to pray for them. Lovingkindness is undeserved royal treatment from the King of Kings.

Day 17: Just the Facts

The concept of God's lovingkindness is not a dream, it's a life-altering fact. You can't be down on life when you're up on the daily merciful acts God sends your way. The truth is, Someone loves you and is committed to you.

God has much to say about the topic of His lovingkindness, but here's a great summary: *Thus saith the LORD, Let not the wise man glory in his wisdom, neither let the mighty man glory in his might, let not the rich man glory in his riches: But let him that glorieth glory in this, that he understandeth and knoweth me, that I am the LORD which exercise lovingkindness, judgment, and righteousness, in the earth: for in these things I delight, saith the LORD.* (Jer. 9:23-24)

Read that again. It's spectacular. If you're smart, strong or rich, that's nothing to brag about. Understanding and knowing the Lord, that He exercises lovingkindness… *that's* something to boast about. And did you catch that He delights in exercising lovingkindness?

His noticeable acts of lovingkindness in your life begin with your salvation. If you have trusted Jesus Christ as your personal savior, and therefore you know you have a right relationship with God because Jesus died and rose again to pay the penalty for your sins, guess what, you didn't grasp that saving concept by your smarts. Remember that previously you were blind, deaf and dumb to what Jesus Christ is all about. He had to take the first step toward you. *The LORD hath appeared of old unto me, saying, Yea, I have loved thee with an everlasting love: therefore with lovingkindness have I drawn thee.* (Jer. 31:3)

God drew you. That's how you acquired the understanding leading to salvation. And He didn't stop there. In fact, He shows lovingkindness to everyone. A person doesn't even have to know Him in order to experience His lovingkindness (though if you don't know Him, you likely won't recognize Him as the source). You don't even have to be a human being to experience God's lovingkindness. *Behold the fowls of the air: for they sow not, neither do they reap, nor gather into barns; yet your heavenly Father feedeth them. Are ye not much better than they?* (Matt. 6:26)

Because I've thought about this a lot, I have some experience noticing how God feeds birds. While sitting in a fast-food drive-thru waiting my turn, I've seen birds dumpster-dive and come up with French fries. I give thanks to God because it's an example of how He feeds them, and I'm worth even more than them to God. He does not neglect the birds, and He does not neglect me or you.

David was probably the Bible person with the greatest understanding of and praise to God for His lovingkindness. Before this section is over, hopefully you can say with David, *How excellent is thy lovingkindness, O God! Therefore the children of men put their trust under the shadow of thy wings.* (Psa. 36:7)

Let's get to the point where we are so sure of God's daily loving commitment to us that any discomfort or disappointment pales in light of it.

Going deeper:

■ Begin now to memorize verses about His lovingkindness, starting with this one: *Thus saith the LORD, Let not the wise man glory in his wisdom, neither let the mighty man glory in his might, let not the rich man glory in his riches: But let him that glorieth glory in this, that he understandeth and knoweth me, that I am the LORD which exercise lovingkindness, judgment, and righteousness, in the earth: for in these things I delight, saith the LORD.* (Jer. 9:23-24) To help you memorize it, visit YouTube for a musical rendition. In YouTube, simply type Jody Shee Jer. 9:23-24.

■ I mentioned that I keep a lovingkindness journal. You may want to consider doing that yourself. How would keeping one affect your life and the lives of others? You can see an example in my suspense novel "The Will of the Enemy" (available from Amazon) Julie, the main character, keeps a journal like this, and it changes her life in interesting ways. Her journal is almost one of the main characters of the book with a life of its own.

Jody Shee
Day 18: Expect Unexpected Love

We've just taken an in-depth look at our lowly, humble condition. That alone isn't going to take us where we need to be in our recovery from depression. In this section, we're coming up for air and focusing more on God and the little favors He likes to show.

You may feel like there's no point praying for God's loving favor, because you know you don't deserve it. Why should He orchestrate an unexpected word of encouragement from a friend you haven't seen in a long time? Why should He provide something you really need today? Why should He draw your attention to a song or book that turns out to be a breath of fresh air at the right time? Well, He does it because He delights in doing those things, and especially to those who know they don't deserve it but expect Him to do it anyway because of who He is. And that's not just wishful thinking on my part. You can be bold and ask God to show you kindnesses, even when you feel like pond scum. Pray something like this... "Lord, I don't know why you would show me a favor of kindness today, but it would preserve me another day if you would just show me your love in some way."

Does that sound weak to you? Good. Because we are weak. David was weak, too. *Withhold not thou thy tender mercies from me, O LORD: let thy lovingkindness and thy truth continually preserve me.* (Psa. 40:11)

But I don't want to completely dismiss the undeserving feeling you might have. If you're thinking, "If only you knew," it might be that there is some sin you are involved in that you know is wrong, but you do it anyway.

You know what you need to do. You need to confess and forsake that sin. It's called repenting. Admit it to God; ask for forgiveness. Come to terms with Him. Ask Him to help you stop it. Cast yourself on Him. *He that covereth his sins shall not prosper: but whoso confesseth and forsaketh them shall have mercy.* (Prov. 28:13)

Whatever you've done, someone else has done it too and gotten victory through confessing and turning to God. Remember David's sin with Bathsheba? He went a little while without repenting. He was miserable. Maybe you are too. But God sent someone to confront him about his sin, and he finally confessed it to God. It may be time for you to do the same. Then pray this with David: *Have mercy upon me, O God, according to thy lovingkindness: according unto the multitude of thy tender mercies blot out my transgressions.* (Psa. 51:1) He wrote that in confession of his sin, and he appealed to God's lovingkindness in that process.

The lovingkindness you might need today is forgiveness, which will certainly bring relief as you restore your relationship with God.

Now, if you are all confessed up and you know you've put your heart in God's hands, determine to stay in fellowship—with His help. Here's a prayer for you. *Quicken* (enliven) *me after thy lovingkindness; so shall I keep the testimony of thy mouth.* (Psa. 119:88)

Going deeper:

■ Pull out your journal. It's time to write. Think back through the past week. What little blessings happened that, at the time, you took them for granted, didn't think much about them or you chalked them up to coincidence. Maybe you saw, heard or read something that was fitting and awesome. Maybe someone did something kind for you. Maybe a circumstance worked out surprisingly perfectly. Maybe someone didn't respond to you in the explosive way you anticipated they would. Maybe a smell or sound brought back a pleasant childhood memory. I could go on and on. Think through the past week and write down all the incidences you can think of. Now, thank God for them. Pray and say, "Thank you Jesus. I'm sorry I didn't recognize it came from you." Then, start watching for more, starting today.

■ Think about this question and find verses to back up your answer: With God, are there any coincidences?

Day 19: Confess His Love

On any day, no matter what kind of a day it is, you can thrive emotionally and spiritually because God has promised to show you little acts of kindness. When you watch for them, you might even think like David did: *Because thy lovingkindness is better than life, my lips shall praise thee.* (Psa. 63:3) He recognized life is OK, but God's lovingkindnesses are even better. (That verse is worth memorizing and meditating on.)

Knowing God's lovingkindness, one morning I left for work without my usual midmorning snack. I always took an apple. But this day, I didn't have any left and no time to stop by the store to buy one. Instead, I thought about God's greatness and asked if He would provide an apple for me at work. I knew I didn't deserve it, but I asked anyway. The more I prayed, the more excited I was to get to work to see how God would provide that little something special. When I got to my desk, I fully expected to see an apple there. But there wasn't one. Instead, I started working, knowing that somehow God would provide an apple. Shortly the coworker who sat across the cube aisle from me came in with a sack and asked, "Who wants apples?" There was my lovingkindness!

I told her she was God's answer to my prayers, and I told her my story. She was equally amazed at how awesome God was to use her to answer my prayer.

Not all lovingkindnesses are so dramatic. It could be that you're in a hurry at the store, and God opens up a parking space near the door. It might be unforseen kindness and attention from someone you weren't expecting. It could be a piece of good news, a victory or a treasured moment. Whatever it is, find a method of remembering, and share your lovingkindnesses with others. Why should you do that?

Because David did it. *I have not hid thy righteousness within my heart; I have declared thy faithfulness and thy salvation: I have not concealed thy lovingkindness and thy truth from the great congregation.* (Psa. 40:10)

I will mention the lovingkindnesses of the LORD, and the praises of the LORD, according to all that the LORD hath bestowed on us, and the great goodness toward the house of Israel, which he hath bestowed on them according to his mercies, and according to the multitude of his lovingkindnesses. (Isa. 63:7)

Rather than being introspective throughout the day, learn to be "extrospective." Start anticipating God's goodness. Trust His promises to show you love. He's great at it and delights in demonstrating it. He also loves it when you give Him credit for it, just as David did. Maybe that's partly why he was said to be a man after God's own heart.

Oh, and one more thing. God's lovingkindness and His mercy are closely tied together. He demonstrates those little acts of love because He is merciful, not because you are so good and special. So you can relax. The word *mercy* implies that you need it, not that you deserve it.

Going deeper:

■ David grasped God's character based on the Scripture he had available to him at the time, which was the first five books—called the Torah, or the law, written by Moses. Study the characteristics about Himself God revealed to Moses in Ex. 34:6-7. It's a passage worth posting in your house. For a printable copy, download the "who is God?" photo from mastertruth.com (under "Free photos").

■ If you've thought of a lovingkindness God showed to you in the past week, share it with someone. It will solidify it in your own mind and encourage the other person.

Day 20: Foreboding or Faith

You wake up and you have a foreboding feeling. Or at least you feel like things aren't quite right. "Ugh. What is going to happen today?" Before you even get up (on the wrong side of the bed), you need a good dose of God's lovingkindness.

His special acts of love really have nothing to do with how you feel or whether or not you're in the right frame of mind. He says: *Nevertheless my lovingkindness will I not utterly take from him, nor suffer my faithfulness to fail.* (Psa. 89:33)

Because God has promised that He is a God who shows lovingkindness, it's perfectly within reason to pray and ask Him to show a lovingkindness—today—based on who He is. How can you know for sure He will answer? *And this is the confidence that we have in him, that, if we ask any thing according to his will, he heareth us: And if we know that he hear us, whatsoever we ask, we know that we have the petitions that we desired of him.* (1 John 5:14-15)

Did you get that? Lovingkindnesses are according to His will, because that's who God said He is. So you can pray for lovingkindnesses and know you will get them. He hears you when you ask for things according to His will.

I have years behind me of praying for lovingkindnesses for myself and for those I love. I don't tell God what the lovingkindness should be (except for the apple at work that one day). I just pray and watch all day. It's called faith. I watch expectantly. *Trust in the LORD with all thine heart; and lean not unto thine own understanding. In all thy ways acknowledge him, and he shall direct thy paths.* (Prov. 3:5-6)

Back to waking up with a foreboding feeling. If you feel that way when you wake up, trade that feeling for a prayer for lovingkindness. Then, rather than look for doom all day, start watching for a gracious gift from God all day. The difference is night and day. And speaking of night and day, consider this: *It is a good thing to give thanks unto the LORD, and to sing praises unto thy name, O most High: To shew forth thy lovingkindness in the morning, and thy faithfulness every night,* (Psa. 92:1-2) The words "shew forth" mean to declare. Before you get going in the morning, declare to God that you know He's a God of lovingkindnesses, and ask for Him to demonstrate it on your behalf. Then, at night, declare His faithfulness, because He did it.

One Sunday, as a single, I came home after church, and rather than eat lunch, I trusted God for a lunch lovingkindness. I waited, for what, I wasn't sure. I watched out the window, and soon a friend pulled into the driveway. She wondered if I wanted to go out for lunch. I certainly thanked God for that, and it's one of many stories I remember because I recorded it in my lovingkindness notebook. The point is, start expecting and watching.

Let your day revolve around your awesome God and not around how you feel.

Going deeper:

■ Practice Psa. 92:1-2 today. (If you're reading this at night, practice it tomorrow morning.) Stop and worship God right now for His gracious acts of kindness and ask Him to show you one today. Then watch for something from Him all day. At night, worship Him for what it was He did for you.

■ Start a new habit of replacing doubt and depression with faith in God's promise to show lovingkindness. Work on your ABC's for Spiritual Health. Are there any verses from the past few days you really want to remember? How about this one for the letter "B" for "better than life." *Because thy lovingkindness is better than life, my lips shall praise thee.* (Psa. 63:3) Go to mastertruth.com and click on "Free photos" to find a verse photo for "better than life."

Day 21: Revival of the heart

As you've watched for God's lovingkindness over the past few days, you likely have seen some that you previously may have overlooked as coincidence. You've heard from a long-lost friend, or someone unexpectedly told you they loved you, and it touched you because you know God put it in their heart. Maybe He helped you find something that was lost. You know what your lovingkindnesses were.

God does these things because He is love, and love gives. His lovingkindnesses are His acts of love. Remember, He so loved the world that He <u>gave</u> his only begotten son, that whosoever believes in Him should not perish but have everlasting life (John 3:16). So it shouldn't surprise us when we see Him act with love in our life and in the lives of those around us—saved and unsaved. God does not reserve His love for those who love and accept Him in return. He causes the sun to rise on the good and the evil (Matt. 5:45).

I point this out because you still might subconsciously think, "Why would He do anything special for me?" Here's why: Because that's who God is. It's not about who you are, but who He is. So learn to go with it and expect Him to be the giving God that He is.

What's in it for God? The praise of His glory. It would be nice if everyone who experienced His great acts of love would praise Him for it. Why don't you be the one? When you recognize God's awesome love, it causes you to glorify Him. In the process, it revives you and makes you want to know and serve Him more.

Only connoisseurs of God's awesomeness will say *Because thy lovingkindness is better than life, my lips shall praise thee.* (Psa. 63:3) Only they will be bold and ask God, *Quicken* (enliven) *me after thy lovingkindness; so shall I keep the testimony of thy mouth.* (Psa. 119:88)

So, remember that His lovingkindnesses are his acts of love that go along with His words of love that we find in the

Bible. In fact, here are some of His words of love: *Yea, I have loved thee with an everlasting love: therefore with lovingkindness have I drawn thee.* (Jer. 31:3) It's His acts of love and His words of love that keep us from falling apart— or we would all be depressed all of the time, because we'd have no hope.

I remember a day in England riding in the car with a friend back to her apartment from an unfamiliar city on an unfamiliar road. Fortunately, she had some written directions, and I was the assigned navigator. "Turn right at the Y ahead," I told her from the directions. When she got to the Y, she panicked. "Left or right?!" she yelled. That made me panic. "Left," I spurted. Oops. I should have said "Right." She was mad at me, and we couldn't find a place to turn around. We kept going in the wrong direction. But soon there was a sign telling us the number of kilometers to our city. What was that sign doing there? So we kept going, and the number of kilometers was getting smaller. Eventually she recognized where she was, and we made it to her apartment. She called the person who wrote the directions to find out how we could have made it back when we went left at the Y. He said, "Oh, my directions must have been wrong. You should have gone left at the Y."

God's lovingkindness orchestrated that scene at the Y in the road. We praised God then, and I still give Him glory today. If you will work on your lovingkindness notebook or computer file, soon you will have a list of stories like that to remember and to share with others.

Going deeper:

God appreciates it when we make memorials of His greatness. My memorial is my notebook. But study these other memorials, like the Jewish Passover (Ex. 13:6-10); the stones Joshua ordered to be set up after the Israelites crossed over the Jordan River (Josh. 4:1-7); and The Lord's Supper that Jesus required be kept throughout the church age (Luke 22:19-20 and 1 Cor. 11:23-26). Can you think of some memorial, besides a notebook, that will help you remember the great things God has done?

Day 22: Vessels for the Master's Use

Today is our sixth day focusing on God's lovingkindness. By now, you are probably aware that if not for God's lovingkindnesses, you would likely be a miserable, hopeless person.

God causes the sun to rise and shine on us each day, and provides sanity in many forms. You've watched for it over the past few days. Now you understand: *In him we live, and move, and have our being.* (Acts 17:28)

Here's another angle to think about. If you look at the lovingkindnesses you received throughout the past five days, didn't some of them come through someone else? It may have been a kind word, a call or text, some information you needed, a hug, a terrific reaction, etc. That person/people were probably unaware that God used them. That's OK. God turns hearts whatever way He wants for the outcome He desires (Prov. 21:1).

Wouldn't it be a delightful thing if you could be the vessel God uses to make someone else's day the way someone else was used by God to make your day? To do that, first determine to live a life pleasing to God, scrubbed of the besetting sins that make you self-absorbed and unable to think of anyone but yourself. *If a man therefore purge himself from these, he shall be a vessel unto honour, sanctified, and meet for the master's use, and prepared unto every good work.* (2 Tim. 2:21)

Look at it another way. God shows lovingkindnesses because God is love, and love is kind (I Cor. 13:4). Do you love others? Then be kind to them. Do acts of kindness. *My little children, let us not love in word, neither in tongue; but in deed and in truth.* (1 John 3:18)

You almost don't even need to pray about it. If you know you can encourage someone else, then make that a goal today. I know the price of stamps keeps going up, and you have a Facebook account, but why not mail an encouraging note to someone? If you see something that reminds you of someone, perhaps you could buy that for them. If you know a lonely single, figure out when you can open up a piece of your schedule and do something with that person.

Interestingly, when you do something kind for someone else, Jesus says it's like doing it for Him. Read about it in Matt. 25:35-40. When you give water or food to the thirsty or hungry, or offer a place to stay to someone in need, or give clothes to a needy person or visit someone who is sick or in prison, Jesus said, ... *Verily I say unto you, Inasmuch as ye have done it unto one of the least of these my brethren, ye have done it unto me.* (Matt. 25:40)

Can you think of someone today who could use something that you can provide?

Going deeper:

■ As you work on your ABC verses to combat depression, how about a "D" word using one of these two verses: *My little children, let us not love in word, neither in tongue; but in deed and in truth.* (1 John 3:18) or the Golden Rule verse: *And as ye would that men should do to you, do ye also to them likewise.* (Luke 6:31) To help you memorize the Golden Rule, visit YouTube for a video (Google YouTube Jody Shee Luke 6:31).

■ Plan something you can do for someone else today to make their day with the following "L" verse in mind: *A new commandment I give unto you, that ye love one another; as I have loved you, that ye also love one another.* (John 13:34)

PART 4: OVERCOMER TESTIMONIALS

In case you learn best by example, this last section is for you. Throughout our lessons so far, I've briefly mentioned the challenges a few Bible characters faced that could have driven them to depression, but they skimmed above it, generally. Let's take a magnifying glass to a few Bible characters. Why? Because we learn from the testimonies of how God works in others' lives.

The testimony of the LORD is sure, making wise the simple. (Psa. 19:7b)

Thy testimonies also are my delight and my counsellors. (Psa. 119:24)

Don't you want to be wise? Wouldn't it be delightful to get the counsel you need free of charge right where you are? That will happen for you by the time you finish this section. Hopefully you will be able to say with psalmist David: *I have rejoiced in the way of thy testimonies, as much as in all riches.* (Psa. 119:14)

Day 23: Fearless Trust in the Lord

No one had better reasons to be depressed or is a better example of how to escape depression than David. He had a lot of drastic episodes in his life that would have kept most of us in bed under the covers curled up in a ball.

David surely must have thought some of his torment was senseless. Consider the vast expanse of time between when the prophet Samuel anointed David to be the next king and when he actually *became* king. Remember this? *Then Samuel took the horn of oil, and anointed him in the midst of his brethren: and the Spirit of the LORD came upon David from that day forward.* (1 Sam. 16:13) Yet it was uncertain years and so many tears before David actually took up his kingly position.

This reminds me of the fact that I've been anointed by the Holy Spirit. I'm a child of the King. I have an inheritance. But there's a long waiting period before actually seeing that inheritance. There's a reason for that: *But the God of all grace, who hath called us unto his eternal glory by Christ Jesus, after that ye have suffered a while, make you perfect, stablish, strengthen, settle you.* (1 Pet. 5:10)

Amazing. My emotional suffering isn't for nothing after all. God works it in me to perfect, establish, strengthen and settle me. You too. David too. He was called, then he was perfected, stablished, strengthened and settled. It happened through trials. The character quality that emerged was a fearless trust in God.

In the Bible, he went from his anointing in chapter 16 to his bout with the giant Goliath in chapter 17. Here are some stand-outs from that episode:

And David (the king in waiting) said to Saul (the king), Let no man's heart fail because of him; thy servant will go and fight with this Philistine. (1 Sam. 17:32) David certainly showed kingly courage.

David said moreover, The LORD that delivered me out of the paw of the lion, and out of the paw of the bear, he will deliver me out of the hand of this Philistine. And Saul said unto David, Go, and the LORD be with thee. (1 Sam. 17:37) Somewhere in his past as a shepherd, David found his life in danger at least twice—once from a lion, and another time from a bear. How about you? God used those animal fights to strengthen David. Now the lesson of "God is able" came back to him while facing Goliath.

Then said David to the Philistine, Thou comest to me with a sword, and with a spear, and with a shield: but I come to thee in the name of the LORD of hosts, the God of the armies of Israel, whom thou hast defied. This day will the LORD deliver thee into mine hand; and I will smite thee, and take thine head from thee; and I will give the carcases of the host of the Philistines this day unto the fowls of the air, and to the wild beasts of the earth; that all the earth may know that there is a God in Israel. And all this assembly shall know that the LORD saveth not with sword and spear: for the battle is the LORD'S, and he will give you into our hands. (1 Sam. 17:45-47)

Let's breathe in some of that confidence in God. David fiercely believed when he couldn't see. He trusted in the Lord with all his heart and leaned not unto his own understanding. In all his ways, he acknowledged God, and He directed his paths (Prov. 3:5-6).

Here, I won't go deeply into the other events of David's waiting period, but Saul was clearly his biggest challenge. Saul continually hunted David to kill him. People problems dogged him. Yet David grew in favor with God and men as he continued to trust God, just like he trusted God regarding Goliath. When David could have turned around and killed Saul (it would have relieved his anguish and hastened him becoming king), he didn't. He trusted God to eliminate Saul. His fearless faith was evident in the things he did (killed Goliath) and things he didn't do (kill Saul).

David, in fact, remained humble and submitted to Saul. He didn't even really challenge Saul as king. He believed that was God's business. He entrusted himself to God, just like Jesus did when he was persecuted. *Who, when he was reviled, reviled not again; when he suffered, he threatened not; but committed himself to him that judgeth righteously:* (1 Pet. 2:23)

If you feel beaten down by a person in authority over you, try to grasp David's mindset. Entrust yourself to God, and let Him work on the person over you. In the meantime, understand that God is using this circumstance in your life for your good… to perfect, stablish, strengthen and settle you.

Going deeper:

■ Today, trust is a great "T" word for your ABCs of Spiritual Health verse list, using Prov. 3:5-6. For a nice frameable photo of this verse, visit mastertruth.com and click on "Free photos." There you will find a link to Prov. 3:5-6 under "trust."

■ Record the insights you gain about total trust after studying these verses: Job 13:15; Psa. 37:5; 125:1; 146:3-5; and Jer. 17:7-8.

Day 24: Be Independent and Dependent

S ome days the tide of unsettling thoughts and events is worse than other days, and you may not be prepared for them, wouldn't you agree? For example, take a look at the time David and his army were away fighting a battle, and when they returned, they found that some enemies had entered their village and taken their wives, sons and daughters captive and burned their village. It's in 1 Sam. 30.

Obviously this was a bad, unexpected day for everyone. *Then David and the people that were with him lifted up their voice and wept, until they had no more power to weep.* (1 Sam. 30:6) Notice that David, the man after God's own heart, is numbered with the men who cried until they were too weak to cry any more.

It was bad enough that David's two wives were among those taken captive. But there was more to his grief: *And David was greatly distressed; for the people spake of stoning him, because the soul of the people was grieved, every man for his sons and for his daughters...* (1 Sam. 6:6a)

So how did he handle it? *...but David encouraged himself in the Lord his God.* (6b)

This shows me that he was independent and dependent at the same time. He was *independent* of his army as they all stood against him right then. That's the case with any leader. When everyone else is down (and down on you), you can't cling to them and sink with them. You have to be the adult in the crowd and lead.

He was *dependent* on God. *He encouraged himself in the Lord his God.* Only when he was independent of everyone around him was he forced to be completely dependent on God, because that's all he had. And fortunately, God is enough. God is the ultimate source of strength, hope and courage.

He had to call to mind all that God is, and he did it alone. Fortunately for us, we know how David encouraged himself in God, because there are Psalms he wrote to show us. He talked to himself. Here are some of the things he said to himself:

Why art thou cast down, O my soul? And why art thou disquieted in me? Hope thou in God: for I shall yet praise him for the help of his countenance. (Psa. 42:5)

What time I am afraid, I will trust in thee. In God I will praise his word, in God I have put my trust; I will not fear what flesh can do unto me. (Psa. 56:3-4)

In God have I put my trust: I will not be afraid what man can do unto me. (Psa. 56:11)

David developed quite the testimony of depending on God. Remember, he was anointed by Samuel to be a king, but it was years before he *became* king. He waited for God to remove Saul, the current king. Remember how Saul chased him and wanted to kill him. Much of David's adult life, he was running for his life. And in the midst of it, we have this story of his own army turning against him. Eventually, David was king and no one was chasing him. But he had developed a habit of depending on God. This is what he later wrote:

And David spake unto the LORD the words of this song in the day that the LORD had delivered him out of the hand of all his enemies, and out of the hand of Saul: And he said, The LORD is my rock, and my fortress, and my deliverer; The God of my rock; in him will I trust: he is my shield, and the horn of my salvation, my high tower, and my refuge, my saviour; thou savest me from violence. I will call on the LORD, who is worthy to be praised: so shall I be saved from mine enemies. When the waves of death compassed me, the floods of ungodly men made me afraid; The sorrows of hell compassed me about; the snares of death prevented me; In my distress I called upon the LORD, and cried to my God: and he did hear my voice out of his temple, and my cry did enter into his ears. (2 Sam. 22:1-7)

David gave God all the credit for any emotional and physical strength he had. He also wrote down his grief and his praise so he and we could read it later—like right now. I encourage you to do the same thing.

All of 2 Sam. 22, David praises God. It's a beautiful chapter in the Bible. *It is God that avengeth me, and that bringeth down the people under me, and that bringeth me forth from mine enemies: thou also hast lifted me up on high above them that rose up against me: thou hast delivered me from the violent man.* (22:48-49)

Going deeper:

■ Can you think of times when you were as low as you could be and God allowed something to happen or for someone to say something that completely shifted your focus away from your circumstance to God's greatness? Write that down as a praise and personal testimony. You need to remember that.

■ Think of a favorite praise song. Stop and sing that to the Lord right now. We will call it a sacrifice of praise. (There are only two times you can praise the Lord: When you feel like it, and when you don't.) In your ABC verse list, consider Psa. 100:5 for your "G" word (good). *"For the Lord is good; his mercy is everlasting; and his truth endureth to all generations."* Listen to Psa. 100:5 on YouTube by Googling YouTube Jody Shee Psa. 100:5. Or, for a colorful, frameable picture of this verse with the word "good" as the key word, go to mastertruth.com, click on "Free photos" off to the right and look for "good."

Day 25: A Testimony of Righteousness

We are reviewing the testimonies God worked in David's life and recorded for us to learn from. Remember, *the testimony of the LORD is sure, making wise the simple.* (Psa. 19:7b)

No matter what you're going through, you want to maintain a righteous personal testimony. Staying between the white lines of God's word will bring that about. And I'm not talking about sanctimonious self-righteousness, but pure, obedient personal righteousness.

It's not popular to be righteous, especially when you're around those who aren't righteous. When you don't join in with them in whatever ungodly activity they are doing, you'll likely hear sarcasm… "Oh, you think you're so righteous." Standing with God sometimes means you'll stand alone. But really, you're in better company. Here's God's perspective: *For the eyes of the Lord are over the righteous, and his ears are open unto their prayers: but the face of the Lord is against them that do evil.* (1 Pet. 3:12)

Most of the time, David was righteous in conduct and character. He was just, fair and stayed within the rules. He is our testimony today of what practical righteousness looks like.

Remember that Saul was king, even though David had been anointed by Samuel to be the next king. David was a king in waiting, and Saul, filled with jealously, tried repeatedly to kill him. You remember that during the chase, one time David found Saul and his men asleep, but David didn't kill him. And then, that same thing happened another time. This time David found Saul in a cave. Rather than kill him, David cut off a piece of his robe. Then he stood in front of Saul and showed him the robe remnant he had just cut off and explained that he chose not to kill Saul, even though Saul was trying to kill him.

David reminded Saul that in no way did he sin against him. *The LORD judge between me and thee, and the LORD avenge me of thee: but mine hand shall not be upon thee. As saith the proverb of the ancients, Wickedness proceedeth from the wicked: but mine hand shall not be upon thee. After whom is the king of Israel come out? After whom dost thou pursue? After a dead dog, after a flea. The LORD therefore be judge, and judge between me and thee, and see, and plead my cause, and deliver me out of thine hand. And it came to pass, when David had made an end of speaking these words unto Saul, that Saul said, is this thy voice, my son David? And Saul lifted up his voice, and wept. And he said to David, Thou art more righteous than I: for thou hast rewarded me good, whereas I have rewarded thee evil. And thou hast shewed this day how that thou hast dealt well with me: forasmuch as when the LORD had delivered me into thine hand, thou killedst me not. For if a man find his enemy, will he let him go well away? Wherefore the LORD reward thee good for that thou hast done unto me this day. And now, behold, I know well that thou shalt surely be king, and that the kingdom of Israel shall be established in thine hand.* (1 Sam. 24:12-20)

It's interesting that it was David's enemy who pointed out that David was righteous, and he didn't do it sarcastically. David chose to trust God to eliminate Saul rather than eliminate Saul himself.

God did reward David good for what he did. He later did become king. David's emotions may have wanted to kill Saul those two times. He could have done it and claimed self-defense.

But here's David's testimony: *The LORD therefore be judge, and judge between me and thee, and see, and plead my cause, and deliver me out of thine hand.* (1 Sam. 24:15).

This is an Old Testament testimony of the following New Testament command: *Dearly beloved, avenge not yourselves, but rather give place unto wrath: for it is written, Vengeance is mine; I will repay, saith the Lord.* (Rom. 12:19)

Years later, before he died, here's how David looked back at that time: *The LORD rewarded me according to my righteousness: according to the cleanness of my hands hath he recompensed me. For I have kept the ways of the LORD, and have not wickedly departed from my God. For all his judgments were before me: and as for his statutes, I did not depart from them. I was also upright before him, and have kept myself from mine iniquity. Therefore the LORD hath recompensed me according to my righteousness; according to my cleanness in his eye sight.* (2 Sam. 22:21-25)

Today's advice is to remain pure and trusting before the Lord, even when you're tempted to take any matter into your own hands. If you're given to anger, let it go today. Entrust yourself to God to judge righteously.

Going deeper:

■ Meditate on this verse from today's lesson*: For the eyes of the Lord are over the righteous, and his ears are open unto their prayers: but the face of the Lord is against them that do evil.* (1 Pet. 3:12) Pray this verse back to God in your own way.

■ The benefits of living righteously before God are awesome and are outlined in Proverbs—written by Solomon, David's son. List the benefits promised to the righteous you see from these verses: Prov. 2:7; 3:32; 10:3; 10:24-25;10:28; 10:30; 11:8; 11:28; 12:7; 13:21; 14:9; 15:6; 15:19; 15:29; 29:6. Note, when you examine the benefits or blessings bestowed upon the righteous, living a righteous life would appear to solve, or at least prevent, a lot of problems.

Day 26: The Art of Bouncing Back

On day 8, we examined guilt and how to handle it when you've done something for which you feel you should probably live banished from blessings for the rest of your life.

If anyone might feel that way, David would be the man, considering his sin of adultery with Bathsheba and the further sin he committed to cover it up. He didn't mess up just a little. He essentially plotted murder against Bathsheba's husband.

If David later beat himself up over these sins, I wouldn't blame him. This is the same David who said in Psa. 119:

(131) *I opened my mouth, and panted: for I longed for thy commandments.*

(143) *Trouble and anguish have taken hold on me: yet thy commandments are my delights.*

(151) *Thou art near, O LORD; and all thy commandments are truth.*

By the way, those commandments include, *Thou shalt not kill. Thou shalt not commit adultery.* (Ex. 20:13-14)

If he loved God's commandments, why did he break them? That's what Nathan, the prophet who confronted David about his sin, wanted to know.

He said to David, *Wherefore hast thou despised the commandment of the LORD, to do evil in his sight? Thou hast killed Uriah the Hittite with the sword, and hast taken his wife to be thy wife, and hast slain him with the sword of the children of Ammon. ... And David said unto Nathan, I have sinned against the LORD. And Nathan said unto David, The LORD also hath put away thy sin; thou shalt not die. Howbeit, because by this deed thou hast given great occasion to the enemies of the LORD to blaspheme, the child also that is born unto thee shall surely die.* (2 Sam. 12:9, 13-14)

His sin allowed the heathen to call him a hypocrite and scoff at God. Before we beat David up any more over this, consider your own life. Have you done anything that has caused unsaved people to shake their head in scorn or bewilderment? Chances are likely, and if it was something horrible, maybe you're still living with the guilt and you find it hard to face God.

But let's assemble the truth that we've learned so far. Don't forget the fact that God is merciful. David wisely knew God well enough to appeal to that when he prayed and asked for forgiveness. Here was his prayer after Nathan confronted him.

Have mercy upon me, O God, according to thy lovingkindness: according unto the multitude of thy tender mercies blot out my transgressions. Wash me throughly from mine iniquity, and cleanse me from my sin. For I acknowledge my transgressions: and my sin is ever before me. Against thee, thee only, have I sinned, and done this evil in thy sight: that thou mightest be justified when thou speakest, and be clear when thou judgest. (Psa. 51:1-4)

And that is today's lesson for how to bounce back from sin. You know better. But sometimes you sin. Instead of dwelling on your inevitable despicable aptitude to break God's commandments, sincerely appeal to God's lovingkindness and the multitude of his tender mercies. He forgives. There are consequences to sin, but He forgives, and so should we.

In the same Psalm, David prayed, *Create in me a clean heart, O God; and renew a right spirit within me. Cast me not away from thy presence; and take not thy holy spirit from me. Restore unto me the joy of thy salvation; and uphold me with thy free spirit. Then will I teach transgressors thy ways; and sinners shall be converted unto thee.* (Psa. 51:10-13)

Like David, believe in God's forgiveness and move on. You may not feel worthy of God's blessing, but quit imagining your unblessableness and focus on the Blesser.

Going deeper:

■ It would be nice to live above sin the rest of your Christian life. But the likelihood of that happening is pretty remote, even for the apostle Paul, who struggled with sin every day. Read Romans 7 and don't stop until you've finished Rom. 8:4. What would you conclude from 8:4?

■ Meditate on these verses on bouncing back: Psa. 27:13; 42:5; Lam. 3:24-26; 2 Cor. 4:8-11 and 4:16-18.

■ Perhaps over time you have become numb to the prospect that you have any sin in your life that hinders God from teaching and touching you. Pray these verses to God today: "*Who can understand his errors? Cleanse thou me from secret faults. Keep back thy servant also from presumptuous sins; let them not have dominion over me: then shall I be upright, and I shall be innocent from the great transgression.*" (Psa. 19:12-13)

Day 27: The Wonder of the Widow

Did you know that God's care for you doesn't depend on you having a sweet, trusting disposition? You can have a crying, painful need that fills your gut with bitterness and despair, and God can and will look upon you with compassion and meet you exactly where you are. His compassion comes from who He is and not from your deserving emotional/spiritual state.

Therefore, it's a mistake to think, "I didn't go to church the past few Sundays, I don't want to talk to anyone, I feel horrible. This Christian life is too hard. God isn't for me like He is for other people."

That's probably something like how the dirt-poor widow at Zarephath felt in 1 Kings 17. When the prophet Elijah met her, she was gathering wood to make a fire to prepare the final meal she imagined she and her son would ever eat. She was cut off from all fellowship with anyone and was completely destitute during a drought, when along came this stranger Elijah asking her if she would make him some food, because he was hungry. *And she said, As the LORD thy God liveth, I have not a cake, but an handful of meal in a barrel, and a little oil in a cruse: and, behold, I am gathering two sticks, that I may go in and dress it for me and my son, that we may eat it, and die.* (1 Kings 17:12)

She was beyond anguish and despair. She had already checked out. The beauty is ... there is a God. Fortunately, He's loving, He cares and He's in control in spite of us.

Go back to the day before. While this woman was probably crying with grief over her sorry circumstances, Elijah was facing his own prospects for starvation. Being a prophet, God spoke to him, *Arise, get thee to Zarephath, which belongeth to Zidon, and dwell there: behold, I have commanded a widow woman there to sustain thee.* (1 Kings 17:9)

Bask in this with me. That widow woman he referred to knew nothing of this plan to feed Elijah that would also sustain her and her son. Yet God told Elijah that He commanded the widow to sustain him. The whole focus of this is God's sovereignty, not her deserving smarts and capabilities.

Elijah did as God said, went and found her and asked for food. She explained how she was planning to make one more meal for herself and her son, *Elijah said unto her, Fear not; go and do as thou hast said: but make me thereof a little cake first, and bring it unto me, and after make for thee and for thy son. For thus saith the LORD God of Israel, The barrel of meal shall not waste, neither shall the cruse of oil fail, until the day that the LORD sendeth rain upon the earth.* (1 Kings 17:13-14)

And so it happened as God commanded. God's provision came to this sorry woman from an unexpected encounter at the perfect time. Do you have stories like that in your life? You may have thought of them when you were reading the Lovingkindness section of this book. Nothing you go through is a challenge to God. He doesn't have a barometer set on your spirit to gauge how closely you measure up to some invisible parameter before He will extend grace to you. He will help you in a snap.

It reminds me of the Saturday, as a single, I sprained my back and laid in bed in the middle of the day, unable to move with no hope of help. The phone next to my bed rang.

It was a lady from church I had barely ever spoken to. She called to see how I was. Odd. I told her, and she said, "Oh you need to see Dr. Shelton. She's a chiropractor. Here's her phone number. Call her. She lives near you, I'm sure she would come over." And so I called her, and she was over to my place in no time. She took care of me that day and over the next several weeks, coming by to pick me up and take me into her clinic for treatments and back home again, because I was in no condition to drive. She was God's lovingkindness dispatched to me in my time of crisis.

Whatever your desperate condition, God sees. He has the solution already in mind. Take courage. He will catch you.

Going deeper:

■ Just how acquainted with you is God? Meditate on these amazing verses: Psa. 56:8; 139:1-18; Prov. 15:3; Heb. 4:12-13.

■ The widow's testimony of God supplying her need reminds me of Phil 4:19 *But my God shall supply all your need according to his riches in glory by Christ Jesus.* That would be a great "S" word in your ABCs of Spiritual Health verse list to memorize. For a 5- by 7-inch photo of it, visit mastertruth.com and click on "Free photos." Scroll down to the word "supply" to find a link to the Phil. 4:19 photo.

Day 28: Elijah Missed Emotional Support

Even Sunday school teachers, Bible study leaders, pastors and pastor's wives have secret sadness they hide. You may be one of them. As the saying goes, it's lonely at the top. The people you lead look up to you as a model of spiritual maturity, so usually they aren't the people you confide in when you're down in the dumps.

Especially for leaders, it's easy to isolate yourself spiritually and emotionally. But if you do that, you'll end up trapped in your personal perspective, which might be off—without you even realizing it.

No doubt you have read about and admired the prophet Elijah, who in 1 Kings 18, stood against the prophets of Baal and challenged them to a fiery show-down between their false gods and Jehovah God. The false prophets were unable to rouse their false gods to send fire from heaven to burn their sacrifice. But in their audience, God responded to Elijah's prayer to burn his sacrifice that was covered in water, just to prove that God could do anything. After a successful burnt sacrifice, thanks to God's answer to Elijah's prayer, he took those false prophets to the brook and killed them according to God's will. Elijah stood for God like few others.

But then there was that wicked Jezebel who heard how Elijah killed all the false prophets and sent a messenger to Elijah to say, *So let the gods do to me, and more also, if I make not thy life as the life of one of them by tomorrow about this time.* (1 Kings 19:2) It was this death threat that sent Elijah running for his life and into an emotional spiral.

A death threat truly is a serious thing, doubly so if the culprit knows where to find you. So Elijah ran away, alone. He didn't tell anyone where he was going. As a spiritual leader, who could he bear his soul to? In his isolated perspective—no one. But wait. Weren't there any other God-followers? He was certain there weren't. We know because when he was talking to the false prophets who worshipped Baal, before he called fire down from heaven, Elijah said to the wicked crowd, *I, even I only, remain a prophet of the LORD; but Baal's prophets are four hundred and fifty men.* (1 Kings 18:22)

This was his isolated opinion. He should have known he wasn't the only prophet of the Lord left, because Obadiah, the God-fearing governor of wicked king Ahab's house, had told him earlier, even before the challenge with Baal's prophets, *Was it not told my lord what I did when Jezebel slew the prophets of the LORD, how I hid an hundred men of the LORD'S prophets by fifty in a cave, and fed them with bread and water?* (1 Kings 18:13)

Elijah wasn't listening, or he didn't care. There were other spiritual leaders just like him he could have conferred with, or hidden with. Instead, we know he ran away and camped under a juniper tree, and when an angel asked him what was going on, he reiterated his incorrect assumption, *And he said, I have been very jealous for the LORD God of hosts: for the children of Israel have forsaken thy covenant, thrown down thine altars, and slain thy prophets with the sword; and I, even I only, am left; and they seek my life, to take it away.* (1 Kings 19:10)

I'm just wondering if he could have saved himself from this depression if he hadn't chosen solitude. He had opportunity for fellowship with other like-minded believers, but he must not have thought it was important.

In some ways, it might be easier to be a lone ranger, but it's not emotionally or spiritually healthy. Start now looking and praying to find spiritual warriors you can confide in, and if you don't see any, pray and ask God to bring some into your life. Believe it when Solomon said, *Iron sharpeneth iron; so a man sharpeneth the countenance of his friend.* (Prov. 27:17)

Going deeper:

Be specific with God when you start praying for godly friends. He is sure to answer your prayer when you pray according to His will (1 John 5:14-15). Meditate on the following verses and pray them back to God in your own way in the context of praying for godly friends: Gen. 2:18a; Prov. 27:9; 1 Sam. 23:16; Ecc. 4:9-10.

Day 29: Abigail Diffused Evil

Sometimes you might dream of isolation if you have a challenging spouse, parent or boss. It is easy to blame that person for making you angry and wrecking your personal peace. You try to walk with God, but then he says, does or doesn't do something that sets you off. It reminds you of the last time that happened, and you anticipate it will happen again and again. Escaping sounds glorious.

Abigail probably wished for a more tranquil, solitary life. Her situation can be summed up in one verse: *Now the name of the man was Nabal; and the name of his wife Abigail: and she was a woman of good understanding, and of a beautiful countenance: but the man was churlish and evil in his doings...* (1 Sam. 25:3)

How does a woman of good understanding handle an abrasive husband? Does she live in tears and run to the neighbor to unload? Does she live in denial in order to cope? Abigail's testimony is remarkable.

In 1 Samuel we read how David's men had occasion to meet Abigail's churlish husband Nabal when David sent them to him to ask for a favor. Nabal spurned them and refused their request. It made David mad, and he rallied his troops to go kill Nabal. But someone told Abigail what was about to go down.

Abigail was not a shrinking violet or an opportunist to ditch her husband. She had her servants prepare some food and went out to meet David and his men who were in route to her house.

Her gift of food stopped David in his tracks. She admitted to David what a jerk her husband was, but implored him not to kill Nabal. She appealed to David's best interest. *Let not my lord, I pray thee, regard this man of Belial, even Nabal: for as his name is, so is he; Nabal is his name, and folly is with him: but I thine handmaid saw not the young men of my lord, whom thou didst send. Now therefore, my lord, as the LORD liveth, and as thy soul liveth, seeing the LORD hath withholden thee from coming to shed blood, and from avenging thyself with thine own hand, now let thine enemies, and they that seek evil to my lord, be as Nabal.* (1 Sam. 25:25-26) She went on to take the blame for her husband and asked for David's forgiveness. She certainly knew how to diffuse a situation.

Abigail was wise in her advice. David wasn't king yet, but she knew that God had promised he would be some day. She explained that it wouldn't look good on his resume if he were to kill a man. (1 Sam. 25:30-31)

Let's soak in a little bit of Abigail. Let's rise up from our pity party and stand for the Lord. How? Don't live according to your imagination. Cast those sorry thoughts away (2 Cor. 10:5). You might have every good reason to live in your depressed thoughts, but start looking at the bigger picture. The fact is, there are evil forces out there that want you to shrink up and blow away. But you don't wrestle against flesh and blood, but against evil powers of darkness with their arrows aimed at your heart (Eph. 6:12). Remember the inner armor you're supposed to put on in Ephesians 6. Abigail had her loins protected with truth. She knew God's plan for David and she knew vengeance belongs to the Lord.

Whatever your emotional state with regards to your spouse, parent or boss, don't allow yourself to wither away. Find the truth that applies to what's going on around you and stand on it.

Going deeper:

■ Read the complete story of Abigail in 1 Sam. 25 and note for yourself the remarkable way she handled the circumstances around her and how God responded in an amazing way.

■ Abigail is said to be a woman of good understanding in 1 Sam. 25:3. What does that mean? For a more complete picture of the phrase *of good understanding*, examine and compare the three other times it is used in the Bible and write your own definition. Psa. 111:10; Prov. 3:3-4; and Prov. 13:15.

Jody Shee
Day 30: God Used Jonah Anyway

It's common when suffering from depression to detach from others and lounge in bed, pull up the covers and go to sleep to escape the turbulence around you.

There's at least one Bible character who demonstrated that. Remember God's prophet Jonah? God's way of giving a message to any people in Old Testament days was to use a prophet to say what He wanted said to a specific group of people. God asked Jonah to go warn the wicked people of Nineveh that if they didn't repent, they would be destroyed. Jonah thought the Ninevites weren't worth saving. He was prejudiced against them, wishing for them to die. He rebelled, refusing to do what God asked him to do. Instead of blessed obedience, he boarded a boat headed in the opposite direction.

We learned on Day 1 that selfishness is a huge cause of depression. Another cause we have not looked at directly is disobedience. We put ourselves at odds with God when we willfully ignore His commands. In the process, harmony with God disappears. When Jonah was on that ship with a group of strangers, he sought peace, not from pursuing God, but from detaching through sleep. *Then the mariners were afraid, and cried every man unto his god, and cast forth the wares that were in the ship into the sea, to lighten it of them. But Jonah was gone down into the sides of the ship; and he lay, and was fast asleep.* (Jonah 1:5)

They woke him up, discovered that God's chastisement was on all of them because of his willful disobedience. *And he said unto them, Take me up, and cast me forth into the sea; so shall the sea be calm unto you: for I know that for my sake this great tempest is upon you.* (Jonah 1:12) At least he owned up to it quickly. They threw him overboard, a whale came and swallowed him, and from that unique position, he repented and agreed to do what God said.

From there, you're familiar enough through the Sunday school coloring pages that are Jonah's legacy to this day, that the whale spit him out on dry ground. Jonah delivered God's message to the Ninevites, they repented and God spared His judgment. God's will and His work were done.

But Jonah's selfishness was not eradicated, just like ours never is. He wasn't happy that God spared the people. He wanted them dead. At least he had the presence of mind to pray. But wait. Look at his prayer: *Therefore now, O LORD, take, I beseech thee, my life from me; for it is better for me to die than to live.* (Jonah 4:3) Because of his inability to align his will with God's, his depression continued.

God knows how to handle us in a way that He knows we will receive, and fortunately, he does it in merciful, non-lethal ways when we probably deserve worse. *And the LORD God prepared a gourd, and made it to come up over Jonah, that it might be a shadow over his head, to deliver him from his grief. So Jonah was exceeding glad of the gourd.* (Jonah 4:6) But overnight God sent a worm to destroy the gourd, and the next day made the day desperately hot. Jonah suffered and grieved again, this time over the dead gourd. God used that whole circumstance to contrast Jonah's selfishness with His compassion. *Then said the LORD, Thou hast had pity on the gourd, for the which thou hast not laboured, neither madest it grow; which came up in a night, and perished in a night: And should not I spare Nineveh, that great city, wherein are more than sixscore thousand persons that cannot discern between their right hand and their left hand; and also much cattle?* (Jonah 4:10-11)

Period. That's how God ends the book of Jonah. The last note is God's and Jonah's contrasting perspectives. It leaves us to ponder many things from the prophet's testimony.

First, God doesn't think like you do. You need a renewed perspective, which you get from listening to and obeying God's commands.

Second, in God's sovereignty, He can and will accomplish His will in your life in spite of you. You can do it happily and obediently, or continue to live dysfunctionally, wishing you could just die. Hmm. Which to choose. I'd aim for a better legacy than Jonah's. The stand-out in his life is not his ultimate obedience, but the whale it took to make it happen.

Going deeper:

Remember, as a Christian you are a vessel for God's use. (On Day 11 we talked about silver goblets.) Jonah wasn't a particularly polished vessel, but God used him anyway. Why is that? Wouldn't God scan the universe for the best vessels to accomplish His perfect will? Apparently not. Study these verses to see how God works with us, in spite of us: Prov. 16:9; 19:21; 21:1; Gen. 50:20; Isa. 14:24; 46:10; Dan. 4:35.

Day 31: Joseph's Dysfunctional Family

Do you have a weird brother, sister, parent or child? I mean someone whose perspectives and actions defy reason. You know what *normal* is, and this person isn't normal. Unfortunately, you become a victim of that abnormality—over and over again. This weird relative probably brings out the worst in you... anger, hatred and the guilt that goes with both, because you know these things are not godly. You wistfully think that if only this person wasn't in your life, you wouldn't feel like this.

Joseph probably felt like that. He had 10 weird older brothers. (We'll let younger brother Benjamin off the *abnormal* hook.) Joseph's brothers were jealous of him and mocked him. After all, he was the white sheep of the family. It seemed he could do no wrong in their dad's eyes.

If mockery was the only challenge of living with his brothers, Joseph's life would have been manageable. But really weird people can even be dangerous, and that was the case with Joseph's brothers. They plotted to kill him. *Come now therefore, and let us slay him, and cast him into some pit, and we will say, some evil beast hath devoured him...* (Gen. 37:20a)

They thought better of that, though. Remember, weird people have a different perspective. They decided that rather than kill him, they would make money off of him and sell him. They threw him in a pit and sat down to eat lunch while they pondered their next move. Meanwhile, someone else with evil intentions came along, drew Joseph out of the pit and sold him before the brothers had a chance to do it.

Imagine if you were in that dangerous position because of your evil family member. It's a travesty. But is it something to slash your wrists over? If there wasn't a God, yes.

Whatever you're going through, it may not seem like it, but God is still sovereign. He will either provide a way of escape (1 Cor. 10:13) or He will work His bigger plan through you in your circumstance. He may bring a ministry opportunity that you can only accomplish if you remain dependent on Him in that circumstance. In your unsavory situation, don't succumb to anger (see Day 2), an active imagination (see Day 9) or the natural feelings that come as a result of bad circumstances (see Day 4).

Joseph had the opportunity to stand for God in the pagan land of Egypt in the house of Pharaoh. God used him and his dreams to provide relief in drought by managing the food supply. This preserved Egyptian lives and the lives of his family, who came to Egypt to get some of that food during the drought.

No matter your circumstances, *They that wait upon the LORD shall renew their strength; they shall mount up with wings as eagles; they shall run, and not be weary; and they shall walk, and not faint.* (Isa. 40:31)

Joseph waited on God and hung in there through good times and bad in his new home—a home he didn't choose.

Then came the family reunion. You know the story. His brothers came to him in Egypt to get some food, for he was the man in charge. They had no idea he was even still alive, let alone that he was the man they were going to have to consult in order to get that food.

God orchestrated that meeting with his brothers. God never forgot Joseph or his roots. Vengeance belongs to God. But you know, sometimes God doesn't choose vengeance. Sometimes He works with mercy. This was one of those times. God preserved these wicked brothers by providing their needs through their brother Joseph.

When the brothers recognized him, they were scared to death. They thought retribution was coming. *And Joseph said unto them, Fear not: for am I in the place of God? But as for you, ye thought evil against me; but God meant it unto good, to bring to pass, as it is this day, to save much people alive.* (Gen. 50:19-20)

Joseph had many choices in how to handle the meeting with his family. In the end, he let the past go. He had already reconciled it with God. He simply moved forward—which turned out to be a gift for his undeserving brothers.

Hang on to what Joseph had—an eternal perspective and the grace to forgive. Trust God's bigger picture. Keep walking with Him, no matter what happens. There's a reward at the end.

Going deeper:

■ In your ABC list of verses for Spiritual Health, Isa. 40:31 would be perfect for your "W" word for the word *wait*. (*They that wait upon the LORD shall renew their strength; they shall mount up with wings as eagles; they shall run, and not be weary; and they shall walk, and not faint.*) For a frameable photo with this verse, visit mastertruth.com and click on "Free photos." Then go to the bottom for the word "wait," and you will find a link to the photo.

■ Maybe you still feel like the bad treatment you suffered through in the past or are currently enduring is more than you can handle. Review 1 Pet. 2:18-23 and meditate on how Jesus handled extreme unfair treatment.

In Conclusion

Whew. You made it through 31 days, and hopefully, you see ways to ditch depression. You may never be completely depression-free. But now you know how to view it. Hopefully, by now you are finished or nearly finished with your ABC list of verses that you can turn to at any time for encouragement in a number of areas. It will be a great tool for you. Instead of listening to yourself, you can talk to yourself using those verses.

Going forward, give God glory. If you belong to Him and He is your Heavenly Father, here's His promise to you: *Being confident of this very thing, that he which hath begun a good work in you will perform it until the day of Jesus Christ.* (Phil. 1:6) He is going to see you through.

If you find that it would be helpful to continue reading short, uplifting devotionals, you can read my blog mastertruth.com, which I update fairly regularly. For a recommendation of other books, see Appendix 2 below.

Appendix 1: How to Have a Personal Relationship with God

My experience with depression dates back to my teenage years when I was plagued with lack of purpose. I wondered what the point was of making it to age 80 or 90, then dying and laying in a grave forever and ever. I know. I was morbid for a teenager. But I know I'm not alone. Like many others, I lived with moderate to severe hopelessness.

Those who are really honest will admit they have a vacuum in their heart—an aching, unfulfilled emptiness. No satisfaction. A search for meaning with no answers.

Some try to fill that void with highs from drugs and alcohol, leading to substance abuse and all the grief that leads to. Others look for fulfillment in friends and love relationships that nearly always sour, at best. Emptiness and lack of purpose or hope is certainly a leading cause of depression.

The first step in overcoming this kind of depression is to realize that you were created by a Creator who wants to be your Father, Guide, Healer, Helper, Stability and Hope. He is God *your* Creator. He made you to know Him, love Him and walk with Him. Are you experiencing that? Maybe not, because by nature, you do not have a relationship with Him. You are separated from Him, living your own life your own way—and it's a hopeless life.

Many verses in the Bible explain the basic problem. Here's one: *But we are all as an unclean thing, and all our righteousnesses are as filthy rags; and we all do fade as a leaf; and our iniquities, like the wind, have taken us away.* (Isa. 64:6) And that's just the way I felt. I was out there drifting on my own, separated from God. I was oblivious to Him. We all are because of our sin.

You will never overcome depression and live an emotionally/spiritually balanced life until you understand this. You need to understand the gospel and apply it to your life. Here are the facts of the gospel:

You have sinned and are separated from God. Even just one sin in your whole life makes you estranged from God. *For all have sinned, and come short of the glory of God.* (Rom. 3:23) Sin is anything that goes against God's commandments—like telling lies, cheating, hating, premarital or extramarital sex, taking God's name in vain, etc.

The price you pay for your sin is death—separation from God now and in eternity. *For the wages of sin is death.* (Rom. 6:23a)

God loves you and doesn't want that eternal separation for you, so He solved the problem of your sin and its eternal-death consequences by taking the punishment you deserve. He came to the earth Himself in the person of Jesus Christ and, on the cross, took your death penalty. As a free gift, He offers forgiveness of sins and a new life by accepting His human sacrifice on your behalf. *For the wages of sin is death; but the gift of God is eternal life through Jesus Christ our Lord.* (Rom. 6:23) Here's another verse that talks about what His death means to you: *But God commendeth his love toward us, in that, while we were yet sinners, Christ died for us.* (Rom. 5:8)

He did more than die for you. He also rose again from the grave three days later, and when He did that, He conquered death. He's alive in heaven right now, and He's preparing a place for you that He offers as a gift.

After you understand the significance and severity of your sin and sinfulness, and after you have grasped that Jesus paid your death penalty when He died on the cross and rose again for you, then you must acknowledge and confess that you are a sinner and receive Him into your life. *That if thou shalt confess with thy mouth the Lord Jesus, and shalt believe in thine heart that God hath raised him from the dead, thou shalt be saved. For with the heart man believeth unto righteousness; and with the mouth confession is made unto salvation.* (Rom. 10:9-10)

This means you will want to pray to Him and admit and confess to Him. Say, "Jesus, I admit that I'm a sinner. I'm sorry. I didn't realize that separated me from you. I understand that you died for me and took my punishment. Thank you for dying on the cross. Now I understand that you did it for me. Please forgive me for my sins and come into my life. I turn my life over to you. I want to turn away from my sins and know and follow you. Thank you for coming into my life now as I accept you. Amen." *For whosoever shall call upon the name of the Lord shall be saved.* (Rom. 10:13)

If you just read and understood all this and prayed a prayer like the one above, from your heart, God answered your prayer and Jesus' death sacrifice was placed to your account. You are now a child of God. You are starting a new relationship with Him. Your goal now is to get to know Him better. How do you do that?

There's a "Fresh Start" e-book on mastertruth.com. Go through that. Also, if there's someone you know who is a believer in Jesus Christ who loves and lives for Him, tell that person what you have done so you can receive their encouragement.

Appendix 2: Other Helpful Books—From My Classics Archives

"Spiritual Depression: Its Causes and Its Cures" by D. Martyn Lloyd-Jones (Wm. B. Eerdmans Publishing Co., 1965)

The 21 chapters in this book are taken from this famous English preacher's sermons at Westminster Chapel. He has some great insights and advice to those who are given to depression. I read it many years ago, and some of his advice is forever branded in my mind. I'm glad it's still available for purchase from Amazon.

"Spirit-controlled Temperament" by Tim LaHaye (Tyndale House Publishers, Inc., 1966, 1994)

I read this book when I first became a Christian several decades ago. The author's premise is that we each have one of four basic temperaments—and usually a combination of a few of them. I saw myself as primarily a "melancholy." That temperament is more prone to depression. The book helped me to understand, accept and learn to work with it.

The book has been updated several times since I first read it. Here is the book description the author has posted on his website: *In this book you will learn how God wants to make you a dynamic, effective Christian who lives above anger, fear, depression, and selfishness. A superb treatment of the basic human temperaments and how God can use them, now revised with new chapters and questions for group study.*

"Joni: An Unforgettable Story" by Joni Eareckson Tada (Random House Publishing, 1978)

This book is especially important to read if you or someone you love has suffered unspeakable pain or grief. *Depression* doesn't even begin to describe what Joni Eareckson Tada went through during her prime teenage years. I was most impressed with how she gradually learned to deal with her circumstances and come through them as one of God's shining stars. She's an example of learning to live triumphantly within your parameters, and everyone has parameters of some kind. Following is her book description:

In 1967, Joni Eareckson Tada was paralyzed from the neck down in a diving accident. In seconds her life changed from one of vigorous activity and independence to total helplessness and dependence. In this unforgettable autobiography, Joni reveals each step of her struggle to accept and adjust to her handicap and her desperate search for the meaning of life. The hard-earned truths she discovered and the special ways God revealed his love to her provide an exceptionally moving story that few readers will finish with dry eyes.

"Do You Hear What You're Thinking?" by Jerry A. Schmidt (Victor Books, 1983)

Much of what bogs us down is nothing more than a misuse of our imagination. We listen to ourselves rather than talk to ourselves. This book gives practical steps for how to replace reoccurring thoughts that lead us down the path of depression (or anger, or guilt, etc.) I read this years ago with a friend, and together we applied the author's suggestions. They worked, and the thoughts that previously plagued my mind went away. I was released from emotional torment. I would wish that for everyone. Get this book.

About the Author

For more than 25 years I've written and edited, first for a book publisher, then for a trade-press publishing company and now as a freelance writer. I write the blog mastertruth.com. After watching the traffic to my blog, I decided to write this devotional. I had a section about depression on my mastertruth home page, and I marveled at how it was by far the most-visited page on my site.

With a passion for writing, I also have a passion for God and the Bible. I studied at Appalachian Bible College in West Virginia, and then finally got my AA degree in Biblical studies from Calvary Bible College in Kansas City, Missouri.

Besides writing for trade publications that go to chefs as a freelance writer, I wrote the fiction novel "The Will of the Enemy" (available from Amazon). My husband Richmond Shee also has written a spiritually helpful book called "The Book of John: A Bible Study & Commentary for Young Believers in Jesus Christ" (also available from Amazon).

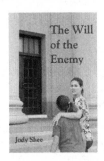

Follow me on Twitter @mastertruths.

If you would like to receive an automatic email when my next book is released, go to http://eepurl.com/G2U-r. Your email address will never be shared, and you will be contacted only for new-book announcements.